60¢

DATE DUE

Ashes for Breakfast

To
Doug, Jack, and our friends
in the witness
at Tattnall Square

Ashes for Breakfast

THOMAS J. HOLMES
in collaboration with
GAINER E. BRYAN, JR.

"God offers to every mind its choice between truth and repose. Take which you please—you can never have both."

Emerson

The Judson Press, Valley Forge

ASHES FOR BREAKFAST

Standard Book No. 8170-0444-0
Library of Congress Catalog Card No. 74-79729

Printed in the U.S.A.

45,881

> . . . I have eaten ashes like bread,
> and mingled my drink with weeping. . . .
> Psalms 102:9

Foreword

WHEN TOM HOLMES SAT DOWN to begin writing this book, he suddenly bent over his desk and wept. The tide of memories, sweeping back, overwhelmed him.

He is not the kind of man who cries easily, nor is he one you would pick out of a Southern crowd as a martyr. To begin with, he is a very tall man, powerfully put together. He is friendly in the outgoing way of the neighborly Southerner — not a purse-lipped reformer, nor a hot-eyed zealot. And in him is the quiet strength and understanding of a faithful pastor who has known a quarter-century of ministry to other people's tears.

But the tears were his own, at last, as he began this simple, straightforward account of a church's ordeal, and his own.

If he had been a weak man, these events would not have happened. Had he been faithless, there would be no story. Instead there would have been just another Southern Baptist Church moving along untroubled from Sunday to tranquil Sunday while the conscience of a congregation slept.

But the Reverend Tom Holmes did have faith and strength to match the times. He believed that any who wish to worship in God's house must be welcomed, black as well as white. Many of his board of deacons and his congregation did not. What then must a pastor do?

This minister preached the truth as his faith revealed it to him. "You are lower down than any dog," a deacon told him. He preached the truth again. And again. At last they fired him.

This gentle believer had no wish to create strife. But he had no way to avoid answering his conscience. Threatened, he stood fast. Repudiated, he declined to retreat. Finally discharged, he would leave only through the front door of a church whose witness he challenged by sacrificing himself.

I saw him and his strong, lovely wife during the months of their ordeal. She told me how much she would regret moving from the pastor's residence in Macon, a house she loved. But her determination was as unswerving as his. Their faith was challenged. They would stand to the end. They could do no other.

In the scourging of a good man for bad reasons there is a Christian lesson considerably older than the crisis at Tattnall Square Baptist Church.

It is a lesson which, well told here, is going to intrude itself in time into every Sunday school room and sanctuary in the South and the nation.

Tom Holmes was not given the time to survive in his ministry, so he was driven from it. But this book tells the lesson with a clarity and a compassion that make it one of the most powerful sermons any honest believer is likely to hear in this troubled American generation. His tears were not for himself.

EUGENE C. PATTERSON, MANAGING EDITOR
Washington Post

Washington, D.C.
February, 1969

8

Preface

My purpose in writing the story of Tattnall Square Baptist Church is to bring to full public knowledge the grievous dimensions of a tragic chain of events which created a sensation in the press of the United States and the world. The story was news because it starkly revealed the contradiction between preaching and practice by Christ's church in the critical and explosive area of race relations. Additionally, the story laid bare the ignominy of ministerial captivity by entrenched power structures within the church which have long fallen behind the thinking of the majority within the congregations — structures whose members are afraid to hear the truth and are determined to prevent their ministers from proclaiming it.

I do not write this book to romanticize my own suffering and that of my wife and family in the sacrifice of my pulpit to deeply held convictions. I do not write to vindicate a personal position that was wrestled to the ground in this controversy.

Rather, I put pen to paper to communicate a message which emerges, I believe, from the painful details of the Tattnall Square Church story. I believe that it is a message of prophetic quality, of both judgment and hope, of breaking down in order to build up.

I address this book to the men and women in the pew and to my brethren in the ministry who together, under God, hold the keys to the church's authority, fellowship, and witness.

Tattnall Square Baptist Church, when I was its pastor, was a typical urban church of the Baptist denomination in the deep South. It differed only in degree from most white congregations of other denominations and other areas of the country. The response that it presented to the critical problem of racial reconciliation confronting churches everywhere was typical. Other congregations need to see their situation mirrored in the dilemma of Tattnall Square Baptist Church. They need to identify and acknowledge their own guilt in the continuance of racial attitudes which are tearing our society apart because these prejudices have not been exorcised from the very house of God.

The tragedy of this church is the nearly universal disgrace of the churches — they might have led the way to community, but, alas, they would not!

The message of this book is that there is yet time for the church to be the church in the modern world. It can yet fulfill its divine commission of reconciliation between God and man, and between man and man. The courageous stand of the Master's minority in Tattnall Square Church, indigenous to the same culture as the majority, points the way to progress and hope in the present crisis. Those who are committed to Christ must stand and suffer, if need be, regardless of the consequences to themselves or the possible shattering of a false peace, in order to be the salt that saves society from decay.

Only as the people of God affirm the basic personhood of all men can they heal the breach between class and race within the fellowship of Christ's church. Only then will they recover the spiritual force to turn the tides of public opinion and conduct into the Christian stream within the nation.

I wish to express appreciation to my wife, Grace, to Dr. Rufus C. Harris, President of Mercer University, and to Mr. Eugene Patterson, who was editor of *The Atlanta Constitution* when the events recorded in this book were occurring. Their encouragement was the dominant factor in my undertaking what has proven to be a very arduous and sometimes painful task of writing and reliving this tragic experience.

Especially am I grateful to Mr. Gainer E. Bryan, Jr., for his collaboration in the writing, rewriting, and editing of this book and for the professional skills that he brought to the task.

My thanks go also to Dr. Benjamin W. Griffith, Jr., of the Mercer faculty, to Mr. Hugh C. Carney, Atlanta attorney who has been my friend since college days, to Mrs. Bernice McCullar, Atlanta author, and to Dr. Oliver M. Littlejohn, Dean of the Southern School of Pharmacy, for their invaluable assistance in reading the manuscript and offering helpful suggestions. To my secretary, Mrs. Louise Meier, I owe a debt of gratitude for typing the manuscript and for the many other services she has rendered.

And to those heroic persons who joined their pastor in this witness, I can think of no more fitting personal tribute than that which Paul paid the Philippian Christians:

"I thank my God for you all every time I think of you; and every time I pray for you, I pray with joy, because of the way in which you have helped me in the work of the gospel, from the very first day until now." (*Good News for Modern Man*).

THOMAS J. HOLMES

11

1

THE SEPTEMBER SUNLIGHT glinted from the ebony face of Sam Oni, African student, as he walked the short block from old Sherwood Hall, men's dormitory, to the church on the corner of the Mercer University campus. A look of calm determination was highlighted in the finely chiseled features of this tall, muscular twenty-three-year-old man from faraway Ghana.

Oni felt himself bound on a historic mission. He was a convert of Baptist missionaries to his country. He had come to Mercer, the Georgia Baptist university, because a missionary and Mercer graduate had guided him there. He was preparing himself for a public service career in his native Ghana.

Tattnall Square Baptist Church, to which he was headed, was one of the churches that had sent the missionaries to his land. This church had voted in the summer of 1966 not to seat Negroes at its worship services. When the pastor and his two assistants had continued to preach and to declare that the house of God should be open to all persons, the deacons had recommended to the church that pastoral services of the three be terminated.

Word of these developments came to Oni in California

where he had spent the summer in study. When he returned to Mercer for his senior year, he felt compelled to go to Tattnall Square because of his unique involvement in the campus and church situation. It was Sam Oni, product of Christian missions, whose application for enrollment at Mercer had broken the impasse between a progressive school administration and a conservative constituency and brought about the integration of the 133-year-old university three years earlier.

During his three years' residence at Mercer, Oni had become familiar with the spiritual schizophrenia of the church in America over the race issue. Shortly after he had arrived at Mercer, the deacons of this very Tattnall Square Baptist Church, dedicated to the service of campus and community, had advised their minister to tell Sam that he was not wanted in their sanctuary. He had been accepted for membership in Vineville Baptist Church of Macon, but only after a grim debate and a plea by their courageous minister that Oni was not an ordinary local Georgia Negro. He was a peculiar Negro, the minister had told the congregation, a unique Negro, one who had come to know the Lord through their own praying, their own gifts, and their own efforts on the mission field.

Sam Oni was going now to Tattnall Square to tell the members that their segregationist policy was torpedoing their own mission program in Africa.

The young foreign student, neatly dressed, knowing impeccable English, fluent French, and three tribal languages, approached the red brick church on the corner of the Christian university. There he was stopped rudely by the ushers of the segregated congregation. They had been instructed to turn all Negroes away, and to these Georgia middle-class white men Sam Oni was just another "nigger." They blocked his way. He asked for the privilege of talking to the deacons or reasoning with them, but the ushers wanted no part of Sam Oni. In their view he had been a troublemaker ever since he had integrated the university and brought integration pressures on the campus church.

When Oni politely insisted that he be admitted, he was seized by two deacons of the church. One applied a headlock on him, and the other dragged him down the steps. Oni kept his cool and did not fight back. He endeavored to reason with his adversaries from the sidewalk.

"Go to the church where you are a member, or some other church," a deacon ordered.

"No," said Oni.

Meanwhile the chairman of the deacons had called the police, who were conveniently nearby with a patrol car. Two policemen appeared in their summer gray uniforms, pistols on their belts, and led the African student to their car. They placed him inside and kept him there until he agreed to leave quietly — while the people inside the church sang the hymn by Frank Mason North:

> Where cross the crowded ways of life,
> Where sound the cries of race and clan,
> Above the noise of selfish strife,
> We hear Thy voice, O Son of man!

Thus was an African Christian rebuffed in trying to enter the house of God to warn his fellow Christians of the disastrous effect of their actions on their own witness. Thus did a white missionary Baptist church reject a child of its own missions. Oni said later, "I couldn't help but remember that Scripture verse which says, 'He came unto his own, and his own received him not.' "

These were the happenings *outside* of the church on the corner of the Baptist university campus the morning of September 25, 1966. They were matched by what occurred inside, which Oni was not able to stop. The congregation voted, 250 to 189, to oust their three ministers.

By these actions the church members denied God's universal ideal stated in Isaiah 56:7 and restated by Jesus Christ in Matthew, Mark, and Luke, "My house shall be called a house of prayer for all peoples" (RSV).

The next day the dismissal of the ministers and the rejec-

15

tion of the African student made headlines throughout the United States and around the world.

To hard-bitten newsmen that was standard man-bites-dog news copy, although the church majority was blind to the inconsistency of their action.

The ministers resigned that Sunday night as ordered, having fought their fight and finished their course, but Sam Oni was not giving up yet on Tattnall Square Baptist Church. "My faith has almost been shattered," he told newsmen at a press conference that afternoon, but he vowed that he would try again next Sunday to attend services and communicate his message to the church.

On October 2, the determined African again was denied admission, but communicate he did — to the church and to the world. He preached a poignant sermon at the foot of the church steps, and the scene and message were carried on national television!

The young man approached the church entrance alone. Two men were waiting at the bottom of the steps. One was an off-duty policeman, a deacon of the church, and the other was an inactive member whom the policeman that day had recruited to help him. Each was more than six feet tall and weighed over two hundred pounds; the deacons had feared that Oni would return this time with a mob. As in his first appearance, however, he refused to let other students join him. This must not be a demonstration, he felt, but a personal stand by a missionary convert from Africa who could not forsake the faith he had been taught by missionaries sent by churches like this one.

The hands of the church "ushers" were not extended for a friendly handshake. Rather the men stood jut-jawed and grim. Their arms were folded across their chests, and when Oni tried to walk around them, they sidestepped to stop him. When he sought to go between them, they blocked him by closing together. Glancing down from their superior elevation, they repeated their statement that the church had decided by majority vote to seat white people only. It was their right, all perfectly legal. After all, can't a Baptist church vote to do whatever it wants to do?

It was then that the rejected African delivered his brief sermon. In calm and measured tones he said, in essence, "Do you not see the inconsistency of what you are doing? You send missionaries to my land to tell me about the love of God, and then when I come to your land I do not find this same love in your hearts. Does God not love in the same way here? Do you not care if my people go to hell?"

Police officers were called again to the church to take Oni away, but when they asked if anyone in the congregation would take out a warrant against him, no one would step forward to do so.

The officers did not talk to Oni that time, and he left saying he would not make any effort to attend the church again. "I have made my point and there's no point in going back," he told reporters. He added, "The world will see what is going on — the empty mockery in that holy of holies."

Summing up, he said later in an interview with the *Baptist Men's Journal*: "I feel that the actions of churches like this repudiate everything that dedicated Christian missionaries are doing. The missionaries you send say to Africans, 'You know why I'm here? You know why I left my loved ones and my home? Because Christ has touched my life, and in touching my life he has given me a burning desire to share with my fellowman — my brothers in Africa — this love.'

"Now, I'll be the first to pay tribute to the missionaries; but what I'm saying is this: Everything that these great men are doing is being repudiated by the actions that are taken here by the churches. But, of course, the churches don't see it. And this is the main reason why I went to Tattnall Square."

One of the paradoxes of the Tattnall Square story is that this church, in rejecting an African student, rejected a part of its founding purpose. The original deed for the church property, however, contained a joker, as we will see in the next chapter.

2

TATTNALL SQUARE BAPTIST CHURCH has had a unique relationship to Mercer University from the beginning. The church was organized in the fall of 1891 by the First Baptist Church of Macon and met in the chapel of the university to minister to students, faculty, and the immediate community. Mercer in a peculiar sense was co-sponsor. The church continued to meet in the chapel for eight years.

A baptistry was constructed in the chapel for the church's use, and eleven converts were baptized there in the first year. When the building was erected, it was on land deeded to the church by the university for the sum of five dollars to provide a church for the faculty and students of Mercer. It was to be a campus church.

The lot was prominently located on the northeast corner of the campus. In compliance with the express wishes of the Mercer trustees the church was built to conform to the architectural style of the Mercer administration building and chapel building.

Reflecting the social concepts of the time, the original deed stated that the membership was to be for whites only and that if the church should attempt to use the property for any other purpose than that of a Baptist church, the property should immediately revert to the Mercer Board of Trustees.

The church got its name from Tattnall Square Park, a two-block square expanse of hedgerows, evergreens, tennis courts, and playgrounds overlooked by the towering old administration building, the chapel, and the church. The other three sides of the park are bounded by residences of the Victorian era.

Beginning about 1900, a very substantial community life clustered around the park. The Victorian homes were centers of gracious living characteristic of the old South. Many of the first families of Macon lived around the park and along the elm-shaded streets that radiated from it. College Street, which ran along one side of the campus and park, connected Mercer, then an all-male school, with Wesleyan College, oldest chartered college for women in the United States. This was one of the most fashionable streets in Macon. The antebellum homes standing today with their magnolia-shaded lawns, white columns, and six-panel front doors bordered by glittering cut glass attest to a former grandeur.

With the completion of the building about 1899, Tattnall Square Baptist Church began to be accepted throughout the community. Many of the old families who had previously belonged to First Baptist Church moved their membership there. For about thirty-five years the church had a stable membership.

During the pastorate of Dr. Lewis H. Wright (1933-45), an excellent preacher gifted in working with people, an educational building was added, and membership grew to almost one thousand.

Two pastors intervened between Dr. Wright and myself. Under the able leadership of these men, and with a new influx of people into the area, the membership grew rapidly until about 1960. At one time it numbered about 1,900. My immediate predecessor led the congregation to complete another building program, and capacity crowds attended services in the enlarged facilities.

19

Tattnall Square Park and Church were situated only about one mile from downtown. About 1955 the trends taking place in inner-city communities all over America began to affect the Tattnall Square community. Many of the old families who had lived in the big houses bordering the park moved away or died. Their children moved to the newer suburbs or left Macon. However, many continued to drive across the city to church.

The fine old homes were divided into apartments, and the more affluent former residents were replaced by lower income groups, many having recently emigrated from farms or small towns to the city. Macon's Negro ghetto encroached on the fringes. Shifts in class patterns brought changes in family life, increases in juvenile delinquency, and other problems characteristic of a disintegrating community.

By 1960 these sociological changes were reflected in the membership and attendance figures of the church. Shrinkage had begun. However, sociology did not account for all of the decline that took place in the church. It was more a matter of attitude and spirit. The members became self-satisfied and complacent. Confronted by an alien invasion of their domain, they turned in upon themselves and became a club for white middle-class persons only. A program of new educational techniques that would have reached the lower class of people moving into the area was rejected, and a decline in membership began. Hardening of the emerging attitudes set in.

Simultaneously, Tattnall Square Church was becoming less appealing to the faculty and students of the university. Gradually, they migrated to other churches, especially Vineville. The Vineville community, located somewhat further from downtown than Tattnall Square, had more successfully withstood the eroding effects of urban changes. The ministers of this church were learned men, and with a more elite congregation, the church maintained a broader world view than its sister church on the campus. Dr. George Connell was a member of the Vineville Church while he was vice-president of

Mercer and continued his membership there when he became president in 1954. The place that had once been held by Tattnall Square Church in the life of the college was largely assumed by Vineville.

By the fall of 1964 the membership at Tattnall Square had declined from its peak by about 450. This rather rapid drop must have discouraged the pastor; in September, 1964, he accepted another position and moved away.

When he left, leaders of the church began to feel that a change needed to be made in the emphasis of the church's ministry in order to regain the ground that was being lost and to forge ahead once more. Some of the leaders wanted to reestablish closer relations with the university community.

These relations had always been harmonious until 1962 when the trustees of the university took an action which opened a breach between Mercer and the ruling powers of the church. Whereas the church, confronted by social change, had withdrawn from the encounter, the university, challenged by the modern world in the demand for racial integration, had taken the initiative. The trustees had voted to open the doors of the school to all qualified applicants, regardless of race, color, or national origin.

Tattnall Square Church was not ready for this decision — few churches of the Georgia Baptist Convention were. No white Baptist church in Macon had opened its sanctuary to Negroes. Tattnall Square's location at the corner of the university campus, however, and its historic commission to serve both campus and community, thrust upon it a responsibility and an immediacy of decision that its sister churches did not have.

In the 1920's a number of Chinese immigrants living in Macon were baptized into the membership. This action, in effect, nullified the stipulation of "whites only" in the original deed, but no one seemed to care enough to make an issue of it, as far as the record shows. The presence of yellow faces in the congregation did not offend the prejudices of the majority. Segregation was scrupulously observed, however, as far as Negroes were concerned. No black-skinned persons were ever admitted to the church fellowship.

The struggle within the Georgia Baptist Convention over the integration of Mercer was one of the top news stories in *The Christian Index,* convention weekly paper, and the secular press of Georgia in 1962 and 1963. Rufus C. Harris, President of Mercer, played a prominent role in the struggle, and I was identified with him in his stand, although much less prominently. From 1960 to 1964 I was Director of University Development and Alumni Relations and Assistant Professor of Christianity at Mercer, having left the pastorate of Northside Drive Baptist Church, Atlanta, to serve my alma mater.

President Harris intensified discussion of the integration issue among Georgia Baptists when he stated as his personal conviction at the annual session of the Convention in 1962 that a Christian institution could not close its doors to qualified Negro applicants. The trustees appointed a committee in January, 1963, to study the issue of integration and recommend a policy. Because letters and other statements of opinion were addressed by Baptists to denominational executives, the executive committee of the Convention appointed a parallel committee to counsel with the trustees. This latter group found opinion so divided and feelings so volatile that it advised the trustees to postpone any change in the university's policy of admissions for the time being. Their report expressed the opinion that Baptists in Georgia were not yet ready for such a change of policy.

Meanwhile, the debate over integration of Mercer moved from the abstract to the concrete when an application from a black student was received. The fact that the applicant was an African, converted to Christianity by Southern Baptist missionaries and guided to Mercer by one of its own missionary alumni, intensified the issue. The president of the university and the trustee committee felt that they were, after all, responsible for the admission policies of the university; that the application before them raised a question of principle; and that they were ultimately responsible to their consciences.

At this juncture they received moral support from an unexpected source. *The Christian Index* came out with a missionary's letter to the editor and an editorial urging that the African student be admitted. The letter was signed by a Southern Baptist missionary to Spain from Georgia, who was at home on furlough. He based his plea on the ethical requirements of the gospel and the necessity of consistency if our missionaries are to be effective in proclaiming the gospel to all peoples. In his editorial, Editor John Hurt called on Baptists to recognize the overriding issue as missions rather than integration — appealing to his readers with irresistible logic.

In April, 1963, the Mercer trustees met and voted the historic decision to admit the first black student to the university.

When Sam Oni arrived in the fall of 1963, the next question to arise was, where would he attend church? A *History of Tattnall Square Baptist Church in Commemoration of Its Seventy-Fifth Anniversary* prepared in 1966 contains this passage: "At their June meeting [in 1963] the deacons discussed the possibility of a Ghana Negro, who had enrolled at Mercer, seeking to join the Tattnall Square Church. The matter was not brought to a church vote and remained unsettled for the next year. . . ." What the history does not reveal is that the deacons counseled the pastor that Oni would not be welcome, and the pastor went to Oni in the men's dormitory and informed him of this fact.

The deacons of Vineville Baptist Church, which I attended with my wife and family, voted to recommend to their congregation that Oni be accepted for membership, should he present himself. He applied there on the fourth Sunday in September, along with about ten other students at the university, all white. Of course, the African was singled out for special consideration although he was admitted as a member.

As the attitude of Tattnall Square Church officials toward Oni became known, many more Mercer students switched their allegiance to Vineville, feeling that its ministry was more relevant to their needs.

3

In October, 1964, I supplied the pulpit of Tattnall Square
Baptist Church on two Sundays and was then called as interim pastor in addition to my duties at Mercer. Many of
the faculty and student body wanted Tattnall Square to become more creative and inclusive in its ministry so that they
could more happily worship and serve there. I was aware of
the tremendous opportunity that a university church has to
guide young people who are in one of the most thrilling,
exciting, and formative stages of their lives. In my preaching
during November and December I challenged the members
to rethink their role as a campus church, as well as a community church, to realize the exceptional opportunity the
church had to help youth find their reason for living and
the will of God for their lives. The congregation responded,
and a new sense of mission began to emerge.

Following the prayer service on a Wednesday evening in
December, the chairman of the pulpit committee, whom I
shall call R. J. (these are not his real initials), asked me for
a conference. We explored the changes that were needed in
the church's approach and my possible continuing role in
helping to bring them about. He revealed his own thinking

that the church should redirect its ministry to include the university community. He also expressed the belief that the members had made a mistake in not welcoming Sam Oni into their fellowship.

I expressed my opinion unequivocally that the church would have to make a very important decision if it was to reach the university community. It would have to be willing to gear its program to minister to all of the students who might desire to come, including foreign students *and Negroes*. R. J. stated that since the church believed in the worldwide mission program of Christ, he could not see any reason why it should not welcome Negro students into the membership if they should want to come. He informed me that people were beginning to ask the pulpit committee that I be approached about becoming the permanent pastor of the church.

I was challenged by the prospects of leading this church back into a closer relationship to the life of the university campus. After all, Mercer was operated by a Christian body, the Georgia Baptist Convention. Tattnall Square Baptist Church was affiliated with that body. The church was thus Exhibit A to the Mercer faculty and student body of the witness of the Baptist denomination.

I felt also that such a church should be vitally awake. It should be aware of all the intellectual currents of our time and should be continuously updating its ministry in the light of the new thoughts, new movements, and new methods of the twentieth century. And it should be creative in its ministries to all segments of the community.

In the ensuing days conversations developed with various people about the possibility of my becoming the pastor, and I informed President Harris of these developments. I told him I would not be interested in leaving Mercer to become pastor of any church except this church. He said he would be reluctant to see me leave the university to go anywhere else, but that we would discuss the matter further if the church became more definite in its interest.

A few days afterward R. J. asked me to meet for a formal conference with the pulpit committee. I stated my convictions that the church needed to minister to all of the students and to create new ministries for the people living in the changing community. The committee was apparently in full accord with my point of view and seemed to feel that I was the logical person to lead in the direction that the members wanted to go. They voted to recommend to the church that I be called as pastor.

On the morning of December 20, 1964, the church received this recommendation and voted unanimously to call me.

As I pondered the call, I thought a great deal about the particular contribution that I could make in the life of Tattnall Square Baptist Church at this juncture in her history. With my years of varied pastoral experience, topped off by five years of service on the Mercer faculty and staff, I dared to believe that God had brought me to the scene "for such a time as this."

I hit upon the idea of a laboratory of practical Christianity which more and more absorbed my thoughts. Because of my identification with the university, I believed we could lead substantial numbers of the student body back to the church. I conceived of a congregation composed of settled, mature Christians mingling with eager young people from the nearby halls of learning, each balancing the other. I visualized a fellowship of concern for the changing community at our doorsteps, with youth and maturity cooperating in a new outreach to people of all classes and races.

Here was an opportunity to prove that these varied people could be bound together in the body of Christ. As the church fulfilled its commission, it could build bridges of communication and cooperation in the community that would assist in its rejuvenation.

The Tattnall Square Church field is representative of a thousand inner-city communities where class, racial, and family patterns are changing. The solutions that we worked out here could be of value in many similar situations throughout America. On the one hand, I could see tremendous problems arising in the congregation as we attempted the task before us. On the other, I could imagine the "well done" of our Lord if we succeeded.

I could see the impact that this exciting program would have on the student young people of our congregation. They would be experiencing the problems that they would soon be facing as business and professional people and homemakers. They would see the relevance of the Christian gospel to all areas of life and would have the opportunity to develop convictions about the adequacy of the Christian faith for every spiritual need of man.

Later our minister to students and I outlined an internship program as part of the overall plan. Many students at Mercer were preparing for the pastoral ministry and for careers in religious education and church music. By adding some of these young people to the staff of our church in an unofficial capacity, we would give them experience that would make their classroom studies more meaningful.

These are the outlines of what I now know was my impossible dream — I thought of it at the time as a challenge to any congregation.

I went to President Harris and told him what I had visualized. The Mercer president is a dedicated Christian and one of the most perceptive men I have ever known. He has had decades of experience as an active participant in Baptist church affairs. Greatly concerned that the church located on the campus should be spiritually challenging to the life of the university, he concurred with my program. After discussing the matter with a number of trustees, he said he was willing to release me to become the pastor of the church.

On the last Sunday of December, 1964, I informed the congregation that I would accept their call on an interim basis and would assume full pastoral duties as soon as President Harris could find a replacement for me at Mercer.

During the early months of 1965 I explored with leaders of the church and university ways in which they could work together to express their common concern for the spiritual life of the students and the youth of the church. As we considered various alternatives, it occurred to us that an expedient would be to employ a person who would serve the church as assistant to the pastor for youth and would work on campus as minister to students. In his campus role he would advise the student religious organizations of all faiths. We hoped by this approach to make the religious life of the campus strongly church-centered.

This plan was worked out in detail, with church and university leaders in agreement. The Rev. Douglas Johnson, then pastor of First Baptist Church of Shellman, Georgia, was chosen for the position. He was a graduate of Mercer and Southern Baptist Theological Seminary, Louisville, Kentucky. A very attractive and able young man, he had had experience in working with youth in Louisville and had been trained in counseling at the Georgia Baptist Hospital in Atlanta. All parties were convinced that Mr. Johnson had the qualifications for the dual ministry.

On April 1, I completed my transition and became the full-time pastor of the church. A few days later Doug Johnson moved to Macon with his wife and four children and began his duties.

In all my thinking and planning about the future of Tattnall Square, I underestimated the depth of the rut the church was in and the entrenched power of several men to keep it there. As I attempted to lay out new pathways of progress, I soon learned who was who in the power structure.

4

IN THEORY, a Baptist church is a spiritual democracy, with the congregation deciding the affairs of the church by majority vote. This, however, was not the case at Tattnall Square.

How this church was governed began to appear at my first deacons' meeting. A young deacon said he thought Tattnall Square should have a monthly business meeting. Surprised, I asked if the church did not have one, since most alert Baptist churches do. The answer was no.

I then asked, "Does the church have a constitution and by-laws?" A middle-aged deacon informed me abruptly that it didn't have, and didn't need any. He spoke with such an air of authority that I gathered he thought he was one of the bosses of the church. In time it became clear that this man, although not the chairman of the board, was in fact the most powerful deacon.

Discussion of a monthly business meeting proceeded anyway. The only church conferences which were held met at the call of the deacons or the pastor, often on short notice, except an annual meeting in the fall to adopt the budget and approve the yearly church letter to the district association.

A motion was made that the deacons recommend a monthly conference to the church and that the board of deacons, department heads, and standing committees submit oral and written reports to this conference. The motion was passed without any open opposition. The very next month a church business meeting was called, the recommendation was approved, and the monthly conferences were begun.

Up to this point the board of deacons had been running the church, quite unlike the usual Baptist form of church government. The all-important church finance committee, for example, had not reported to the congregation, but to the deacons, who then decided what to tell the congregation. The church members never heard the full report. Although resistance to a monthly church conference was not openly expressed, the decision to hold one regularly was a challenge to the power of two men who were dominating the board of deacons and, through it, the church.

The identities of these two men were revealed to me as I attempted to lead the church in a progressive program. What triggered the disclosure was a speech that I made about the shabby condition of the sanctuary. At a deacons' meeting I suggested that the central worship area of the church needed a face-lifting. The carpets were worn. The floors were loose. Many of the pews were rickety. The plaster was peeling. Lighting was totally inadequate. Pigeons were getting into the sanctuary through holes in the steeple.

After reviewing these conditions, I suggested that the deacons take a look for themselves, discuss what they found with other members of the congregation, and consider drafting a recommendation to the church.

The next afternoon R. J. met me in the sanctuary as I was taking a short-cut through the building. He was one of the three-member board of trustees, whose responsibilities included care of the church property.

"Pastor," he said, "I want to talk with you a few minutes."

"All right, Mr. R. J.," I replied. So we sat down on the long pew running across the back of the auditorium.

Noticeably agitated, he spoke in this vein: "I hear you have presented to the deacons a matter that is going to involve a large expenditure of money. I want you to get off to a good start here. I don't want you to make any mistakes, and I think you have made one. If you do anything to this sanctuary, it's going to require a large expenditure of money, and before you make any recommendations concerning the spending of large amounts of money, you ought to talk to two or three of the men privately."

I replied, "Well, I don't want to make any mistakes. I thought I was following good Baptist procedure to take this matter to the deacons. To whom should I have talked?"

He was very reluctant to specify any names, but as I pushed him for this information, he finally identified two: his own and that of another deacon, whom I shall designate by the initials D. K. Having thus made clear who the church bosses were, he plunged to the heart of the issue at hand. "I don't think we need to do anything to this sanctuary," he said. "This building is all right. I have been worshiping here for years and years, and I don't see anything wrong with it."

Clearly, R. J. was one man who would have to be convinced before anything could be done about the shabbiness of the church plant. He had never really made his way through the entire sanctuary. On Sundays he had the habit of slipping through the right rear door into a chair in the nearest corner, and that was as far as he got. Looking primarily at the choir and the ministers, he had failed to notice overall conditions.

I said, "Mr. R. J., will you just sit here while I turn on the lights, and then let's take a little tour." I guided him over the dilapidated premises. What he saw shocked him visibly. There were seventy-nine pieces of glass broken in the beautiful stained-glass windows. The frames of some were rotting, and the sashes were in danger of collapse. In many instances the screws had pulled up through the bases of the pews, causing them to sway and creak as worshipers

31

stood or sat during the service. There was a hole in the floor of one of the aisles where a woman's heel could go through the carpet and floor. Pressure on several loose boards produced loud squeaks. I pointed out the cracks in the plaster and the peeling of the wall paint.

After this inspection tour, he left, with few comments. The next morning, however, I received a call from him. "Pastor," he said, "I have a confession to make. I hadn't noticed the condition of the sanctuary before. I went downtown and was talking to one of my friends about it. He said to me, 'R. J., you sit there all the time. It's home to you. You've grown accustomed to these conditions. Your new pastor is a stranger, and he would be more likely to observe the actual situation.' "

He was obviously concerned now. He clearly wanted to see the house of the Lord kept in good repair. He concluded, "Go ahead and get a committee. Let's raise the money and fix the sanctuary. This church has always done whatever was needed, and we will do it this time." I asked him to serve as chairman of the committee, and he readily agreed, with the stipulation that a vice-chairman be named to do the talking in public because R. J. disliked that role. Also, his health was not good.

Now that R. J. had approved the idea, my recommendation that the sanctuary be redecorated was easily passed at the next deacons' meeting. It was then presented to the church at the monthly business meeting and approved unanimously. What this episode demonstrated to me was that the basic decisions of the church were not made by the congregation. They were in the hands of two men who jealously guarded their power over the purse strings and the policy-making.

After several months spent in studying the community and the possibilities of the church, I realized that we should have a long-range planning committee. I discussed this with the deacons and gave them a month to think it over. Their recommendation to the church to set up the desired committee was unanimously adopted.

In spite of the surface harmony, opposition to the forward movement of the church, the realignment of its ministries, and the new interpretation of its role was developing. From my brushes with the power structure, I concluded that either R. J. or D. K. would have to take the chairmanship of this committee if the effort was to get off the ground. With R. J. already heading the renovation committee, that left D. K. as the prime candidate for the other post. So I approached him with the proposition.

On my first visit he asked for time to think it over. He stalled the second time I went to him. My third time at bat I struck out — he refused. It looked like the end of the ball game, as far as long-range planning was concerned. No other person in the church would accept the leadership if D. K. balked. Greatly disappointed, but not defeated, I decided to play the waiting game, hoping that in time the younger progressive members in the church would assert themselves. I moved for the implementation of my program in small chunks instead of as a whole.

It was obvious by the spring of 1965 that we were going to have a large attendance of students. Their numbers grew steadily from fifty to seventy-five to one hundred at the Sunday morning worship service. Even fifty was an increase over that of the preceding five or six years. From time to time I emphasized that we should seek to minister to *all* the students in fulfillment of the mission of the church; that we should never make any distinction by choosing to accept some and not others. Unless we made it obvious to this generation of students that "red and yellow, black and white" were included in our concern, we would lose the ones we had.

At that time there were twenty to twenty-five Negroes enrolled at Mercer. Although only four or five lived in the dormitories, it was possible that some might desire to attend our services, and I did not want them to be turned away. I felt the church should face the issue and prepare for this eventuality. Once again the procedure of appointing a study committee to recommend a policy seemed to be appropriate.

This committee would have to be a strong one. Its stature and the content of its report would have to be such that the congregation would see their duty and perform it. There was only one conclusion that the group could make if the members considered the matter in the light of Christian ethics, the lordship of Jesus Christ, and the leadership of the Holy Spirit. This was to welcome all persons who desired to come to the house of God to worship — regardless of race, color, or national origin.

Mindful of the power structure, I went straight to D. K. this time and asked him if he would make the motion in the deacons' meeting to establish this committee. To my surprise, he readily agreed to do so. This seemed too easy to be a genuinely progressive move, but it was something. At the meeting I brought up the matter, D. K. made the motion, and it breezed through. The church later approved the recommendation, but there the project simmered.

According to the motion, the chairman of the deacons was to appoint this committee, but he dragged his feet. I asked him two or three times when he was going to name the panel. His repeated answer was that he was trying to find "strong leaders" who had made no public statement of their position. This task was impossible, for what leader had not made his position known?

At long last he appointed five people to serve, the majority of whom could be expected to preserve the status quo. They met shortly afterward. I was not invited to attend or even informed of the meeting in advance. No one asked me for resource materials. No report was made to the church or the deacons. I later learned that the committee merely reviewed the great responsibilities assigned but refused to budge off dead center, even at the urging of the two progressive members. The group met again several weeks later but took no action. They did not meet again until almost a year had passed.

What stymied the committee was a quiet campaign by segregationists in the church to block any move toward opening our doors to Negroes. It was widely suspected that D. K. had advised the chairman of the committee not to call any more meetings. One of the weapons the segregationists used in their campaign was a deceptive rumor based on a legal fiction.

The fiction was that the Tattnall Square Church was legally prevented from the admission of Negroes by the old reversionary clause in the original deed. As stated earlier, the deed of the lot from Mercer University had specified that the church to be erected on it was to be "for whites only" and that if the facilities ever ceased to be used for a church, the property would revert to Mercer. The rumor was that the pastor's desire to open the doors to blacks was actually a clever ruse to "steal" the church property for Mercer. This story was given great credence by many who knew better. It spread throughout the congregation and played on the fears of the older members, especially.

Upon hearing this rumor, I went to our church attorney and asked to see the deed. After reading it, I decided that the best course would be to get a legal opinion on the validity of the reversionary clause. I asked the attorney to write President Harris giving him the full story and requesting an opinion from the university's attorney.

This was done. The Mercer attorney, T. Baldwin Martin, stated that in the light of the university's revised racial policy favoring integration, the reversionary clause could not now be enforced even if desired. I was satisfied, but I did not publish this correspondence since I did not want to enlarge the issue. This information should have been given to the special committee, it is now clear, although the chairman probably would have kept it to himself.

The church did a splendid job of raising the money to redecorate the sanctuary, primarily through special offerings at Easter and Thanksgiving, 1965. Through a welter of committees the work proceeded. A personal friend who was an interior decorator suggested a beautiful color scheme, without charge. Volunteer labor was unselfishly donated. We repaired the beautiful old oak pews, cleaned the woodwork, painted the walls a subdued gold, installed indirect lighting and Gothic lanterns, put down a gold wall-to-wall carpet, and repaired the lovely, classic stained-glass windows. The traditional Gothic sanctuary assumed a new dignity and fairly glowed with beauty.

These changes had a marked effect on the spirit of the congregation. The members responded with a newfound pride in their house of worship. Students and young marrieds demonstrated a renewed interest.

Jack Jones, instructor of music at Mercer, became our part-time minister of music, succeeding a Mercer student who had graduated in June. Well educated, he was a brilliant concert organist and an inspiring teacher and director of choirs. Under his mentorship our music improved steadily, but a number of people were unhappy. Some did not like sharing their minister of music with the university. Some felt his selections were too difficult and "high-toned." Despite the obstacles, Jack won the affection of most of the people, and there was definite progress in the music department of the church.

Despite the good response to the redecoration project and the improving music, the better attendance at worship services, and increasing involvement of youth, an undercurrent of opposition was forming. It is often difficult for a minister to know just where he stands. So what happened at a deacons' meeting in the fall of 1965 was a shock to me.

Doug Johnson had begun to grasp his responsibilities as assistant pastor and minister to students and was outlining a vigorous program. He had begun to make plans for the use of the educational building for various student religious activities during the week. After consultation with me, he had drawn up some recommendations to be presented to the deacons at their next meeting. These called for the use of two large assembly rooms as well as some classrooms in the educational building for vespers, committee meetings, and other student activities. We wanted to make the church a center of student religious life and to provide meeting places that were not available on the crowded campus.

When this matter was presented to the deacons, there was silence for some minutes. Then came a veritable avalanche of rejection. In short order, Doug and I realized we had absolutely no chance to win approval of this idea from the deacons.

Some utterly astonishing comments were made. One deacon voiced the bugaboo that Roman Catholics might be among those using the building; another, that Episcopalian students might hold drinking parties on the premises. Mercer University prohibits even the possession of alcohol on the campus.

Their reaction clearly indicated that the majority of the deacons were wedded to the status quo. Their spiritual horizons were so limited that they could not make available to any except Baptists their church facilities that were largely idle during the week. This reaction showed Doug and me that we were in for a battle every step of the way as we tried to lead these people to carry out their total mission.

There was another fracas in the spring of 1966 which indicated that opposition to a progressive administration was hardening. Douglas Johnson, in his work with youth, arranged a spring retreat at Toccoa, Georgia, for young people, ages 13-16. In an effort to relate to the life needs of these teenagers, Doug scheduled a series of discussions on a "Christian View of Sex." When the young people came home, several complained to their parents about Doug Johnson. Their alleged dissatisfaction was about the sex talks. They said the discussions had embarrassed them. The result was that some of the parents of those complaining attacked Doug, even suggesting that he resign.

Open discussions of sex were not new to our teenagers. There had been such a forum at a retreat a year earlier, and then only appreciation of Mr. Johnson's efforts had been expressed. Doug had asked all of the young people to write evaluations of the encampment and had saved the papers for me to read. A perusal of these reports uncovered a hidden cause of the young people's anger against Doug. He had insisted on "lights out" at 12 o'clock and had prohibited boys from visiting the girls' quarters and vice versa. Although denied, this was the real source of their resentment.

As the uproar grew, Doug and I invited all of the parents involved to a meeting to air the whole matter. When the full story was known, the parents, for the most part, conceded that Doug's discipline was what had provoked the resentment and that his efforts to help our youth obtain a biblical view of sex were helpful.

There were a few, however, who let their anger smolder, and it became obvious to all that their objections fitted into a larger pattern — they belonged to the "loyal opposition."

One of the most discouraging aspects of the pastoral ministry is the fact that the pastor cannot lead his church by the simple process of offering Christian principles that should govern the church's life and ministry. He must deal with entrenched power groups that often are motivated by factors other than Christian principles. He must descend to the level of catering to selfish interests, inflating human pride, and engaging in political maneuvers within the church in order to circumvent small minds and spirits.

The discovery of this reality has been the undoing of many a young minister who has compromised his integrity as a man of God to achieve what is called success in the modern church. Earlier in my life I had done my share of that sort of leading, but it had produced a sense of shame and a spiritual crisis in my life. I came to believe that such compromise is one of the basic reasons for loss of spiritual vitality and moral character in both ministers and churches.

Before I went to Tattnall Square I had decided that life is too short for me to stoop to the methods of ward politics to accomplish the church's business. However, I reckoned without the stumbling blocks and intrigues encountered at Tattnall Square.

The real conflict began when Doug Johnson, Jack Jones, and I decided that we would challenge our people, not with sophisticated pastoral coddling, but with the imperatives of God's Word. Not only was our program at stake at Tattnall Square, but our integrity as Christian ministers. We chose to preserve the latter if one of the two had to be sacrificed.

I learned of a project that the Second Ponce de Leon Baptist Church of Atlanta had conducted in the winter and spring of 1966 called "Operation Involvement." Its success in rallying the people and deepening their spiritual commitment had been dramatic. I secured printed information on this program and distributed it among our deacons. After due consideration they voted to ask the church to undertake a similar program, beginning in September, 1966. A general chairman was appointed, and he began preparations in June.

To support this effort, I decided, after conversations with the deacons and staff, to preach through the book of Acts during the summer. This wonderful and thrilling book is most relevant to conditions confronting the church today. My objective was to show how the early church, encountering problems within and without, struggled toward realization of the universality of the Christian gospel.

On the first Sunday in June I began this series of sermons. That experience was one of the most exciting and challenging of my life, with many hours spent in study, meditation, and prayer. After nearly thirty years as a minister, I was experiencing, as though for the first time, the tremendous excitement and struggle of those early Christian brothers. Reliving their experiences, retracing the steps of their pilgrimage with them knit a sense of kinship between a present-day pastor and those men of old. I sought to lead my congregation to discover the radical nature of New Testament Christianity.

It will never be known what dedicated leadership and an imaginative program could have accomplished in the renewal of this once great, but tired, old church, because the issue that was dividing American society moved to center stage at Tattnall Square. To the segregated church, forewarned but tragically unprepared, the showdown eventually came with the appearance of unwelcome visitors.

5

DURING THE 1966 SUMMER SESSION, Mercer University, in co-operation with the Federal Office of Economic Opportunity, had an Upward Bound Project. This was an enrichment program for deserving young people from underprivileged homes. It brought 100 juniors and seniors from the high schools of middle Georgia to the campus. As in all federally financed projects, the Upward Bound program was open to all persons without regard to race, color, or national origin. So about half of the enrollees were Negroes.

The project's director inquired as to churches that would be open to the racially mixed young people. Douglas Johnson was asked about Tattnall Square, and he came to me for guidance before replying.

I knew that the inevitable showdown over the church's traditional policy of segregation was drawing near. The special committee that the chairman of the deacons had appointed to recommend a policy for contemporary conditions had not reached a decision. D. K. had maneuvered to nullify any recommendation that would change the status quo.

In the interim the chairman of our deacons had instructed the ushers to seat any Negroes who came, but he had no church action to back up his ruling. I had made my personal position clear: I could never say to any student or other person that he could not attend the church because of his color. With the issue thus unresolved, I was painfully aware of the possibilities for controversy should any of the Negro students attend our church.

I asked Doug to explain our situation fully to the project director — we could not *invite* the Negroes to come, under the circumstances, but if they should come, they would be seated.

It may be asked, why didn't I call the deacons together and fully inform them of the possibilities of Negro visitors? The answer is simple: They had been told on several occasions that this was inevitable. I had asked the chairman of the deacons repeatedly to talk with the special committee chairman and urge him to act. On my third approach he had angrily replied that he had appointed the committee and that was as far as he would go — he was not going to involve himself in a controversy. I had tried by my preaching to change hearts and attitudes.

As I look back upon this landmark decision, honesty compels me to reveal a deeply disturbing conviction of those days. In early America the people faced a spiritual crisis when Jonathan Edwards came under divine conviction and preached his famous sermon, "Sinners in the Hands of an Angry God." In 1966 I was burdened by the thought that the people of God in America had become *unloving Christians in the hands of a loving God.*

Our myths of centuries had at last caught up with us in the historical situation. Did we really intend to follow the implications of the good news of a God who loves all men equally? Could we be serious about a universal brotherhood of believers in Christ? Would we support by our practices the men and women who had gone to distant lands to preach the gospel? Could we honestly demonstrate to the adherents of non-Christian religions that we had anything superior to offer them?

As far as Tattnall Square Church was concerned, it was at last face to face with its destiny. Its members had long contended that a congregation had been placed on the Mercer University campus by divine appointment and this fact had been attested by a potent influence on the life of the university in the years past. Yet when Mercer, after three years of agonizing self-examination and acrimonious criticism, had struggled to meet her moral obligations in the changed world of the 1960's, the church had refused to accept its responsibility. By causing the pastor in 1963 to inform Sam Oni that he was not welcome, the power structure had placed both pastor and church in a humiliating posture from which neither could easily recover.

Now the moment of truth had arrived. Do not the circumstances of who we are, where we are, what we claim for ourselves, and the commitments which we follow, ultimately thrust us into encounters with the Divine from which we cannot escape? I believe this is what happened to the pastor and people of Tattnall Square Church, for it is the only Baptist church in Georgia located on a Baptist college campus and Mercer University was the first Georgia Baptist institution voluntarily to accept Negroes as a policy demanded by its Christian purpose. Though the church was free to chart its own course, it was folly to believe that a church so situated could minister relevantly without accepting responsibility for its total constituency.

Though I did not precipitate the confrontation between black visitors seeking an opportunity to worship God and a segregated church determined to be a respecter of persons, under a sense of divine compulsion I refused to try to prevent it. Just as I could not prevent the confrontation, I could not stave off the judgment that inevitably followed.

Now with the crisis upon us, I took only one more step. I spoke to several ushers whom I knew to be reasonable men. I notified them of the probability that Negro students would attend a service and asked them to be available to handle the situation. That was on Wednesday, June 22.

Doug conveyed our message to the project director. At 9:30 on Saturday night, June 25, Doug telephoned me to say that he had been informed that several Negro students had expressed a desire to attend our church the next morning. They would be accompanied by their counselors, senior students in the university who often attended our church. My reply was, "So let it be."

After making several telephone calls, I went to bed and slept well, surprisingly, realizing that the morrow might well be one of the most crucial days of my ministry, and certainly a day of crisis for my congregation. My only prayer was, "Lord, help us to conduct ourselves as Christians should." I left the matter in God's hands.

Eleven o'clock on Sunday morning has been called the most segregated hour in America. That tradition was broken at Tattnall Square that particular Sunday, for at ten minutes before eleven, June 26, the assistant pastor told me that there were two Negro students in the congregation of Tattnall Square Baptist Church. He said they were accompanied by a student counselor and his fianceé.

My heart always pounds as I await the moment to enter the pulpit for a worship service. With the report that Doug Johnson had given me, it pounded harder than usual! As he and I walked into the sanctuary, I saw that it was filled almost to capacity. I couldn't detect any marked difference in the people's faces. In fact, many of them didn't know the Negroes were there since these visitors had taken seats near the rear of the sanctuary. Five people left the room after the opening prayer, but otherwise there was perfect decorum. I merely welcomed all visitors as usual.

My sermon that morning, continuing my series from the Book of Acts, was from the third chapter, the passage which tells of Peter and John healing the crippled beggar at the Beautiful Gate of the Temple. My text was, "Then Peter said, Silver and gold have I none; but such as I have give I thee: In the name of Jesus Christ of Nazareth rise up and walk." My subject was "Such as I Have I Give."

The message was simple. There are needy people all about us if we will but see them. We all have something to give which others need. Christ gives us many gifts that we are blessed in sharing. As Christians we must share with anyone who is in need.

When the service was over, I stood at the rear door to greet the people as usual. Not a word of protest was spoken as several hundred persons came by to speak to me. I shook hands with the two Negro students and welcomed them to our church. They expressed appreciation for the service. They were treated cordially by many people. Not an unkind word was spoken to them. It seemed we had passed a crisis in fine style.

However, after the congregation had left and I was on my way out of a side door, I was accosted by the rather high-strung wife of a deacon. She was angry and near tears. She asked me if I had known the Negroes were coming. I told her about Doug Johnson's call at 9:30 the night before. She then insisted that the pastor should have informed the deacons about the call and implied that they would have acted to prevent the Negroes' attending. I didn't argue with her because she was obviously upset.

The point that she raised was repeated and repeated by dissident members of the church in the days following. I was accused of having deliberately deceived the leaders of the church.

My wife, Grace, fully shared my ideals and the ordeal through which I was passing. She had learned to love black people as a child in the middle Georgia village in which she was reared. She had seen the plight of impoverished Negro women who had worked in her mother's kitchen and had yearned to help them, to show that she cared. As an expression of her concern she was teaching remedial reading that summer in the predominantly Negro Meta Danforth School, which had the first integrated faculty in Macon.

She relates, from her vantage point in the pew, the drama that unfolded on that crucial Sunday morning.

"Tom asked me if I would sit with the black student visitors if they came. I was happy, even excited at the prospect. Perhaps they would bring new life in our church, I thought. I asked Annette Highsmith, one of the most radiant Christians I ever knew, the widow of a Mercer professor, to sit with me. She said she was eager to do so. Tom arranged with Dr. Ben Griffith of the Mercer faculty, who was vice-chairman of the board of deacons, and Mrs. Griffith to sit in the pew ahead, in case there was trouble and we needed assistance. (The chairman of the deacons was out of the city during this incident and for several days following.) These arrangements were made the night before.

"Annette and I were very excited as we sat down on the fourth pew from the front. People were arriving through the various doorways and moving in different directions to their seats. We watched the doors and the ushers but never did see any Negroes come in.

"The choir, resplendent in new green robes, filed into the chancel. Tom and the other ministers, dressed in dark suits according to Baptist custom, entered from side doors and took their places at the pulpit. The auditorium was aglitter with its new traditional Gothic light fixtures, new gold-green carpeting, and matching freshly painted walls. The sanctuary was up-to-date in its decor, but anxiety gripped my heart as I realized that our congregation was not up-to-date in racial attitudes. I wondered if Tom's stand and the actual appearance of Negroes would result in our having to leave this church and the pretty parsonage in the Northwoods which was our only home.

"The service began and I still had not seen any Negroes enter. Annette and I began to whisper to each other, 'Do you suppose they came and were refused entrance?' I said to myself, 'If they've been turned away, I will leave, too.' I had long felt that I would not be willing to be a member of a church that denied entrance to Negroes.

"The music and the prayers were completed. Tom arose to preach. I sat through the entire sermon in suspense and

45

pathos. The seats beside Annette and me remained empty, as did those beside the Griffiths. We came to the end of the service without anything unusual happening, so far as I could tell. When we stood for the benediction, Annette and I began to whisper our questions to each other again. I looked around and to my amazement, saw two black teenage youths about three rows behind us, turning to leave a crowded pew. They were neatly dressed in black trousers, immaculate white shirts with long sleeves and black ties, but no coats. Trying not to attract the attention of our parishioners beginning to speak to me, I spoke softly to Annette, 'Turn around, Annette, look behind us!'

"Irrepressible as a child, she said, 'Let's go speak to them!' For a moment, I held back, fully aware of what it might cost Tom and me thus to identify myself with the black visitors. If I refrained from speaking to them, I might continue safe within the white kingdom.

"I saw the strangers being swallowed up by the crowds as they went out the main entrance. And I made my reckless choice. I would speak to them, but I wouldn't make myself conspicuous by cutting through the crowd. So I said: 'Annette, let's go out the back door and meet them on the side as they head back toward Mercer.'

" 'All right,' she said, and wheeled around on her crutch, for she was crippled. But when we got outside, they were nowhere in sight. So we *ran* toward the front, I in my high-heels and Annette on her crutch bouncing along, the flowers on her tan pillbox straw hat bobbing up and down. We ran past our parishioners, not stopping to shake hands, for fear the young men would get away before we could greet them.

"By the time we got to the front sidewalk, the whole congregation was clustering there to talk with one another. The two youths were crossing the street. Annette reached the line of parked automobiles, threw up her free arm and called: 'Boys, hey, wait!' They stopped and turned around. She shook their hands, told them how glad she was they'd come. And I, trembling, did the same, extending my arm over the corner of the gleaming blue hood of a late model car. I said I hoped they'd come again. In reply to my questions, they told me their names and where they were from.

"They left, and I became conscious of two parishioners whom I had not seen. A particularly important couple had entered the blue car at the curb beside me and witnessed my handshake with the black visitors. Now they fixed me with a cold, hard stare. I tried to greet them as though nothing unusual had happened, but their disapproval was obvious.

"As Tom and I drove home, I had a foreboding that the hurricane was about to strike."

6

I WAS SUPPOSED to go to Atlanta in the afternoon to assist two pastors in a funeral service for a dear friend of many years. Grace and I were several miles up the highway when our car developed engine trouble. After some delays we had to give up the trip and return home. To our surprise, we didn't receive any telephone calls that afternoon. We now know that this was only because the people thought we were in Atlanta. They kept the wires hot calling one another, however.

That evening we were to have the commencement program for the Vacation Bible School. I left for the church about six to finish preparations for the program which was presented by the teachers and the children in each department. Soon after I left, Grace received a phone call from a woman posing as a newspaper reporter.

"I hear the Nigras attended your church this morning," the woman said. "Is this true?"

Grace was immediately on guard. She replied, "Yes, they did."

Then her caller said, with anger in her voice, "I understand that you shook their hands. How did you feel?"

Grace replied, "I don't think that's anything to get excited about. It happens often. I teach black children at school, eat with them at recess. And the sky hasn't fallen in."

The caller hung up. Grace was certain that it was no newspaper reporter. Only six hours had elapsed, but the harassment had begun.

At the church service there were many parents present with their small children who demonstrated what they had learned in Vacation Bible School. I was made doubly aware of the inconsistency in our racial policies by two participants in the program. They were two little Korean girls. Their beauty, intelligence, eagerness, and lack of self-consciousness drew much attention from the congregation. Their father, a professor at Mercer, and their mother were present. Although certainly not white Anglo-Saxon Protestant Americans, these people were welcome at our worship services and Vacation Bible School, but blacks were not!

After the service was over, Grace and I were walking through the sanctuary toward the exit when we were accosted by a group of four deacons and their wives. One of the men, a slightly built, bald-headed, normally mild-mannered and courteous person, blocked my path. I will call him Rayford Brown, not his real name. His face was red with anger. His lips and his hands were quivering. He blurted out, "I want to tell you just what I think of you." I paused and waited for the verbal blow. "You are lower down than any dog I have ever known," he rasped. "I can't tell you how low-down I think you are. You are through as pastor of this church. I'm going to lead a movement to throw you and Doug Johnson out."

He paused to get his breath, then resumed the attack. "You think you staged a scene here today. You haven't seen anything. You just wait until next Sunday; I'll show you something. I know how to handle things like this."

Rayford had been an excellent churchman and a good friend of the pastor. He often did jobs on church equipment that saved considerable money. To say I was shocked by his attitude is not quite true. What was surprising was the vehemence of his attack. But many times I have seen normally composed people lose all reason when the race issue arises. It's the most emotional question in the South. My greatest surprise came when he suggested he might attack me physically — "I may be smaller than you, but you don't scare me," he said.

I replied, "Yes, you are small." This was an unchristian remark, for which I later apologized. I was holding my temper reasonably well but was determined to meet this threat and not be intimidated by any individual or group.

"You should think twice before you create a scene in the house of God," I advised him. "As long as I'm pastor here, the doors will be open to anyone who desires to worship. This is the Christian gospel as I understand it."

My wife and I were shaken by this confrontation. We drove home in silence. The gauntlet was down, and both sides knew it. We were in the eye of the hurricane.

The phone was ringing as we entered the house. Some callers told us of their support and prayers. Others, angrily refusing to give their names, accused me of betraying them and my calling as a minister. Some may not have been members of our congregation. We could see the church cracking open like the earth in a mighty earthquake.

Grace left early Monday morning for her school. I had a study at home and was there alone when the phone rang. It was the wife of the deacon who had accosted me after the service Sunday morning. Her call was designed to bring pressure to bear upon me. She said, "Dr. Tom, we sure would hate to lose you from our church."

My reply was, "You are not going to *lose* me. I'm not planning to leave."

"I want to tell you something else," she said, "a lot of people are mad at Grace. They're saying she shook hands with the Nigras but wouldn't shake ours." What she meant was that Grace should have shaken their hands and ignored the Negroes.

She then related how she had told a former pastor, when he preached on the race issue, that he had better change his views. She said, "The pastor thought it over and decided that he wasn't going to mention the matter again."

I cannot vouch for the truth of that incident, but I decided to let her know that her tactics were useless with me. I replied, "Whatever action any other pastor took in this matter is none of my business. But as for me, I have struggled to rid myself of prejudice and I know what God expects *me* to do. I will never be a party to turning any worshiper away from the house of God."

As soon as she had hung up, the phone rang again. It was a Sunday school teacher in our church. He said, "You know where I was raised — in Johnson County, Georgia. I was raised on prejudice, but the Lord has helped me to get rid of it. I hear they are going to try to vote you out. I just want you to know the vote to fire you won't be unanimous." This was the first definite warning that I received of what was to come.

Prejudice and agitation were exploding all over the city. It was becoming difficult to be calm and rational.

The chairman of the deacons was in Des Moines, Iowa, for several weeks. I learned that he had made plans to call a deacons' meeting on the Monday night following any visit by Negroes. Deacons were phoning Ben Griffith, vice-chairman of the board, in the absence of the chairman, insisting that the meeting be held that night. He called me to ask my advice. He did not want to call a meeting, and neither did I. We were both of the opinion that some time to "cool off" was needed by all. So he did nothing.

D. K. was demanding a meeting, however, and he refused to give up. Bypassing Ben Griffith, he telephoned the chairman of the deacons long distance and secured a telegram authorizing a meeting, which he scheduled Tuesday night, June 28. The meeting was not to be an official session, and no recommendation of any kind was to come from it. It was to be a time of prayer and discussion.

On learning this news from Ben I drove to his home Monday night to talk it over with him. We decided that I should call the chairman and discuss the whole matter with him. The chairman and I had been on the most cordial terms when my pastorate began, but he seemed to resent the diminished powers of the deacons as time passed and I had found it difficult to communicate with him for several months. In our conversation he stated that I had allowed the Negroes to attend knowing that it would divide the church. I reminded him that the special committee which he appointed had had nearly a year to act, that he had refused to prod them to action, and that the church had received no leadership from the deacons which would have prepared them to accept this inevitable situation. He was reminded firmly that much of the responsibility for the violent reaction then dividing the church was his.

With Dr. Griffith presiding, the deacons' meeting was attended by about thirty-five men. It was opened with a period of prayer in which a large number of the men participated. During the three hours of discussion all of the old arguments against "race mixing" were aired. Against them was posed the question, "What would Jesus do?" The answer was obvious, but the problem was that most of the deacons did not seem interested either in knowing or in doing what Jesus would do. Their ignorance or disdain was striking.

A deacon arose to read a published sermon by the pastor of a nearby church. The selection which he read was positively segregationist. The deacon's conclusion was that this scholarly preacher was much better informed than I was and had stated the case in irrefutable logic.

D. K. now played his "ace in the hole." He came to the front bringing a copy of the church's deed from Mercer, dated 1893. He read the clause stating that the church was to be for whites only and asserted that the laws of Georgia prevented us from admitting Negroes to our services. If we did so, he declared, Mercer had a legal right to demand the church property. The implication was clear: namely, that

Mercer coveted the property and that I was a tool of the university trustees to seize it for them. By his speech he revealed that he was the originator of the rumor which had been making the whispered rounds for months.

Then he finished and sat down, with a look of evident satisfaction, confident that his position was unassailable, and that he had vanquished the opposition. Unknown to him, we had anticipated this stratagem, done our homework, and were ready with the rebuttal. Our church attorney came forward. He revealed that he had known for months about the innuendo directed at Mercer and me and had written to President Harris requesting a legal opinion on the reverter clause. He then quoted from the letter of Attorney T. Baldwin Martin to President Harris, dated January 31, 1966. The sum of the university attorney's opinion was that Mercer could not enforce the reverter clause even if she desired to do so, because the school had changed its policy from segregation to integration. Thus there was nothing to the rumor of a Holmes and Mercer plot to steal the church property.

We thought this had settled the matter once for all, but we learned too late that the deacons had neither understood nor absorbed the legal reasoning of the attorney. The rumor continued to be circulated.

Some of the deacons raised the question that the deacon's wife had asked — why didn't the pastor inform them of the developments that led to the visit of the Negroes? I answered in three parts. First, the chairman had already established the procedures to be followed. Nothing else could be done except to refuse to seat the black students, and the deacons had not decided to do this. Second, I had repeatedly warned the deacons and many others that Negroes were bound to come sooner or later; I did not know when. Third, when I finally understood that a visit was probable, I did notify three deacons including the vice-chairman and several ushers and ask them to be at the doors to seat the Negroes if they came.

Veiled threats of dismissal were made against Doug Johnson and me. Time proved they were more than threats; they were statements of intention.

When every deacon who wanted to had spoken, Dr. Griffith asked me if I had anything else to say. I went straight to the heart of the matter. With no anger or belligerence I said, "You have been honest with me. I am going to be equally honest with you. I want you to know that I am not frightened by the things that you have said and implied here tonight. I do not plan to resign. I am not going to retreat an inch from the position I have taken. I have arrived at this position slowly, deliberately, and prayerfully over the years of my spiritual pilgrimage. To change now would be to deny past spiritual experience. I cannot be a party to denying any person the right to enter God's house and worship."

I told them I loved them in spite of any differences of opinion we might have. I emphasized the importance of calmness and reason and pled for harmony that would preserve the church and move it forward.

When the meeting was over, some of the tension was gone, but I could not believe that the matter was settled. I decided to ignore personal harassment and vilification, to make no reference to any of this from the pulpit, and to continue my program of preaching as previously announced.

The wives of several deacons formed teams of two who were constantly visiting the membership and agitating the matter. What their husbands would not do openly, they did with a relentlessness and thoroughness that was amazing. They did it with no regard for the integrity of the church or the truth of their statements. I was constantly astonished at the bizarre interpretations that were given to my sermons and the utter distortion of my motives.

Isn't this always the case when willful opponents cannot destroy the truth? Their only recourse is to destroy the person who speaks it. This they now seemed determined to do. However, I was to win the first round by a vote of confidence.

7

From June 26 to July 17 the fire smoldered. On Sunday morning, July 17, I had finished my sermon, the last hymn had been sung, and I had bowed my head to pronounce the benediction when I heard a loud voice from the congregation, "Brother Pastor," the speaker said, "I request that you call this church into conference. I have a matter that I want to bring before the congregation." The member speaking was a handsome, black-haired attorney now graying at the temples, a straight thinking, fearless individual who could never remain neutral in great issues. Though his move was unexpected, I asked quickly if there was any objection to hearing him. There being none, I called the church into conference. He walked up the steps to the pulpit, and I took a seat on the front pew and waited to hear what he might say.

The emotions that were battling within him were immediately apparent. With a slightly choked voice he began, "I wish that I did not have to do this, but my conscience will not permit me to be still. Our church is in a great crisis. We stand at the crossroads. We will either go forward now, or we will retreat into oblivion. Our pastor has preached the truth to us. He is now under attack for his views and for allowing two Negroes to attend our services.

"I have heard rumors that the deacons are going to ask for his resignation when they meet tomorrow night. (This was news to me). I think that this congregation has an obligation to inform our deacons as to how we feel about our pastor. They should not consider such a crucial action without knowing your feelings. I, therefore, move that we give our pastor a vote of confidence."

His motion was immediately seconded by several men and women. I was completely taken by surprise. Never in my life had a vote of confidence been taken for me. In fact, in twenty-five years as a pastor, this was the first controversy involving me in which my leadership was the bone of contention. Although embarrassed, I had no choice but to allow the congregation to vote. The action was so sudden and fast-moving that it did not occur to me to withdraw and let someone else moderate the conference. The lawyer put the motion to the church himself.

The vote was overwhelming in favor of confidence in the pastor and his leadership — 300 to 18, as nearly as could be determined. I arose from the front pew and thanked the people and asked them to pray that we would follow the spirit of Jesus in this crisis. Then I pronounced the benediction. Grace came down to join me at the front and we stood there to speak to the people, not going to the rear door as usual.

The lawyer's information was accurate. There was anger on the faces of several of the deacons which would be explained on Monday night. Their plan of action had been formulated, and the "skids were greased" to discharge all the ministers at that meeting. No action would then have to be taken on seating Negroes, and the church could return to the status quo. It would be a double play and the end of the ball game, the power structure probably figured.

The vote of confidence by such an overwhelming number had shaken these deacons to their toes. In spite of the carefully spread slanders and innuendos of a grand plot between the pastor and the Mercer officials, the congregation was almost solidly behind us.

As I reflect on the whole chain of events, I must conclude that this vote of confidence was a definite turning point. It forced the leaders of the opposition into the open. But it did more: it forestalled our immediate discharge and established a bridgehead of support that made our long struggle possible.

The deacons met on the Monday night following, and the first order of business was a motion to request the resignation of Doug Johnson and Jack Jones. The chairman of the finance committee had an elaborate argument prepared in which he endeavored to show that the church could save money by discharging these two men, who had dual responsibilities, and by employing one man full time. He referred to the tenure of the student who had combined the ministries of music and youth. This arrangement had worked fine, he now claimed. I could not help remembering that this deacon had been one of the most relentless critics of the former arrangement and a leading advocate of employing Doug Johnson. He had said at that time, "Preacher, this church is ready to go. All we want you to do is tell us how to do the job."

Jack Jones was on leave that summer studying in New York, but Doug Johnson was present to listen to the speeches cataloging his alleged failures and those of his colleague. The critics studiously avoided attacking me, but their strategy was obvious: if they could discharge Johnson and Jones, they felt certain they could get my scalp, too. I was revolted by the obvious untruths in much that was said.

The former secretary of the deacons, now inactive, was present. I thought this strange but decided that the chairman of the deacons must have asked for him to make a report as chairman of a special committee on nursery and kindergarten work. The inactive deacon had often posed as being appreciative of Doug Johnson's work, but I had seen him equally critical of it. He arose, gained recognition by the chairman, and went to the lectern. Pulling several sheets of paper from his pocket, he began to read a prepared speech.

It was a harsh attack on Doug Johnson. I was so astonished and incensed that for several minutes I didn't know what to do. Doug sat with his eyes on his accuser and with great dignity answered not a word. I decided that this tirade was going to be stopped. This man had no right even to be at the meeting, although the chairman had allowed him to come and to speak.

I arose and interrupted the speaker. I said, "Brother Chairman, may I ask a question?" The chairman replied, "Yes, sir."

"Is this brother an active member of this board?" I asked. The chairman stammered a moment, then answered, "No, sir, he is not." I then asked, "May I ask if he is here by invitation, and, if so, by whose invitation he is here?" Then the member of the board who made the motion to discharge Johnson and Jones spoke up and said, "I asked him to come." The whole matter was so completely out of order and shameful that a very painful silence ensued, and the speaker was motioned to his seat by the chairman. After the meeting I sharply rebuked the speaker, telling him that he had no right to be present, and that his attack on Doug Johnson was unchristian and his charges were untrue.

Another incident occurred that was most revealing. R. J., who was not on the board, also attended the meeting. He was asked by the chairman to speak. He professed his love for the church and told how his heart was broken. He made the statement that we all must rid our hearts of bitterness.

All the while he was looking straight at me. He was angry with me because on Thursday of the week before I had met him, at his request, for a talk in the lobby of the Dempsey Hotel. His concern at that time was the divided condition of the church. He had said then that the pastor could bring the church together again *if the pastor wanted to.* His clear implication was that I must forsake my position and come to D. K.'s view and his view. I reminded him of the things he had said to me prior to my call as pastor. He made no reply but insisted that I should change my position "for the sake of the church."

I stated that he and D. K. could reconcile the factions in the church if they wanted to. He said that he had been accused of running the church. I told him I had heard that he and D. K. had done so for years, but that they were not going to dictate to me in a matter of conscience, and that I had no intention of surrendering. R. J. used the word "bitterness" to characterize my attitude; but what he mistook for bitterness was merely my stubborn refusal to submit to his desires.

He then began to weep before the deacons. When he gained control of himself he made a statement that left me speechless. He said, "Our pastor promised me before he was called to this church that he would never let anything like this happen" (referring to the visit by the Negroes). This was the precise opposite of what I had said. I had warned him repeatedly that one day the Negroes would come, without any assistance from me.

R. J. had a heart condition and now was in a highly disturbed emotional state. I had to make a quick decision. If I challenged this misstatement and provoked him into having a heart attack, I might be accused of killing him. I decided to make no reply but to depend on the memories of the deacons and the records of the pulpit committee and discussions in previous deacons' meetings to reveal the facts of the matter. Little did I realize that my silence at this time would be interpreted as secret agreement with him, and that this would be used against me in a church conference at a later date.

After others had spoken, some in defense of Doug and Jack, I arose to defend my young associates. I quoted statistics that demonstrated the truth to their critics. I realized that we were risking the ruin of the church, and I warned the deacons not to wreck the church and deny its great tradition of challenging youth to Christian service. I reviewed our history. I reminded the deacons that of the fifty alumni of Mercer University who were serving on Baptist mission fields around the world, twenty-five had been members of Tattnall

Square Baptist Church. At least some of their inspiration for Christian service had come from this church. A number of students had been ordained to the ministry at Tattnall Square. If the church were to be led on a reactionary course to close its doors to Negroes, the youth in the membership would not recover from it and the Mercer students would avoid the church.

D. K. made no speech at this meeting. He must have felt that he could win or he never would have allowed the vote. When it was taken, the motion to dismiss Johnson and Jones was defeated by one ballot, eleven to ten. Immediately someone made a motion to remove the previous motion from the record and to make no reference in the minutes to this whole discussion. This motion passed. It was the first time in my life that I had ever heard of such an action. It spoke to me of cowardice and shame. One could not help but think of Pilate's action in washing his hands when he had delivered Jesus to his crucifiers. But, fortunately, men cannot deal with history so cavalierly.

After this action, the chairman called the chairman of the special committee on racial policy to report. Never have I heard an angrier tirade than this committee chairman delivered against the attorney for calling for the vote of confidence the previous Sunday morning. (The attorney was not present at the deacons' meeting as he was not an active deacon.)

The whole sequence of events then fell into a pattern. The committee had met on the day before and had voted three to two to recommend to the church that the doors be closed to Negroes. I was not notified of this meeting, so this was my first knowledge of the committee's recommendation.

When the committee chairman presented the report, he did the strangest thing I had ever seen such an official do. He explained that the vote in the committee had been two to two and that he had broken the tie by voting to close the doors. Then he made a long and emotional plea for the deacons to reject the very report of the committee which he had passed and *not to vote for closing the doors!*

60

Was this a ruse to appear to be on both sides when the time came to accept responsibility for his vote before the congregation? Was it a belated recognition that to adopt the report would wreck the future ministry of the church, perhaps forever? Or was this report simply a bluff and a part of an attempt to induce our resignations and then take no action on the issue, thus returning the church to the moral vacuum in which it had lived for years? I am certain that the opposition felt at this time that they could survive this crisis if they could only get rid of us. I believe they were hoping that enough roadblocks would leave us so discouraged we would resign.

I had determined that I would not resign, and had been joined in this course by Johnson and Jones. The vote of confidence the day before had given us some hope that the obstructionist deacons might relent and change their course. However, they were so used to dominating the church that they concluded they could still win in spite of the great majority I received in the vote of confidence.

Hundreds of southern churches had pressured ministers with racial views like mine to resign quietly and slip out the back door. These churches had thus avoided the glare of publicity revealing their unchristian machinations. Then they had gone on in their evil course. Often they had blacklisted their former pastors for all future years.

At whatever the cost, I refused to go out the back door. The principle of human rights and the freedom of the pulpit are too important not to make a fight for them. If church leaders are determined to reject the universal gospel and to crucify their ministers who are committed to preach the truth, they must bear the consequences. I had the feeling that I was not fighting for my position alone but for the moral leadership of all pastors similarly threatened. Without freedom of the pulpit there can be no spiritual progress in the church. I determined to see this struggle through. The battle lines were now trenches!

It was after eleven o'clock when I got home from the meeting. Grace and Annette were waiting up for me, eager to hear what had happened. When I'd finished with the sorry news, Grace and I decided to go to see Doug and Joy to try to give comfort. We found them in tears in their living room. Doug was sitting at his desk, sipping coffee. The sorrow and trouble that had come to this lovely young family was one of the most distressing aspects of the whole controversy to me. To realize that Grace and I could do no more than share our love and sympathy with them was most frustrating.

8

THE DEACONS ADOPTED the report of the special committee and
recommended it to the church for approval. They set July 24
as the date for congregational action, the meeting to follow
the morning worship service. It was further decided that the
vote would be by secret ballot. The ballots would be numbered; they would be signed by each voter and checked against
the membership roll. Then they would be counted by tellers
selected by the chairman of the deacons and myself, and de-
stroyed. The chairman and I were instructed to write a letter
to the members and inform them of the committee report, the
recommendation of the deacons, and the voting procedure.

I had no confidence at all that the recommendation would
be defeated. I could have tried to delay the vote, hoping for
a change of minds on the issue, but decided not to. Baptist
churches have operated for centuries under the belief that the
congregation rules. In fact, Baptists have practically substi-
tuted the doctrine of congregational infallibility for the doctrine of papal infallibility. Too often votes are taken by a
congregation with very little thought given to their ultimate
consequences. Apparently, the whole controversy had progressed to a point of no return. The power structure had

undoubtedly decided that they would settle the issue by a conclusive vote and then we would resign and the church would return to its "normal" life.

Many southern congregations of other, more centralized denominations had chosen wiser courses. Their leaders had decided to open their doors, receive any Negroes who might come (uninvited of course), prevent any unpleasant incidents, and then be in a position to cooperate with inevitable social change. These leaders know, as I do, that racial justice is a part of the new day which churches must accept or else be cast aside. Under this sort of strategy, dialogue can be promoted that will prevent great upheavals but still facilitate the necessary adjustments in an orderly fashion.

This was the course I had recommended for nearly two years, but it was rejected by the leaders of our church. Their fears of change, their confirmed prejudices, their "all or nothing at all" philosophy, snared them in a web of circumstances that ruled out reason and compromise. The history of Baptists will reveal that many hundreds of new congregations have been formed from minority groups driven from their churches by precipitate actions and polarizing votes. Despite the folly of misguided majorities and the tragedy of church splits, a slow and tortuous forward motion has resulted. This is one explanation of the multiplicity of Baptist sects.

The segregationists in the church did a thorough job of preparing for the vote on July 24. A large crowd was present. I estimate that there were at least one hundred people in church that Sunday that I had never seen there before. It is likely that most of these newcomers voted to close the doors to Negroes.

My sermon was a character study of Stephen, the first martyr. It was not planned to coincide with the showdown in our church, but was in the sequence of my series of sermons on the book of Acts. I had already done all one could reasonably do to present the Christian course in this issue, but my conclusion to the sermon was that Stephen died a martyr to his conviction of the universality of the gospel.

When the service was over, I called the church into conference, explained the parliamentary rules that would govern any discussion of the resolution from the committee and the deacons, and asked for restraint and Christian fairness in any debate. After answering questions concerning the ballot and the mechanics of the vote, I opened the floor for general discussion. The deacon chairman quickly made a motion to shut off all debate on the grounds that minds were already made up, the issue was settled, and any debate was useless. The motion was approved unanimously. It was just as well, because emotions were unbelievably strong. Any objective consideration of the real issue was impossible. The congregation then proceeded to ballot, after which the benediction was pronounced, and the long drawn-out procedure of checking and counting the ballots was begun. We went home without knowing the results.

The longer I live the more I realize the importance of a good family life to mental and emotional health. The crisis of that day was the greatest Grace and I had ever experienced. Our daughter and her husband had driven to Macon to be with us. Our son and his wife also spent the day in our company. Coming also to share the ordeal and lend moral support were Grace's brother, Gainer Bryan, Jr., and his wife, Mary Anna.

We tried to be cheerful as we ate Sunday dinner. I felt the undergirding of love and common commitment. We carefully avoided the expression of our fears, that the vote might mean that the battle to admit Negroes would be ultimately lost.

About two o'clock in the afternoon the phone rang. It was the superintendent of the Sunday school on the line. "Pastor," he said dolefully, "the church voted 289 to 109 to close its doors to Negroes." He said that every ballot had been carefully checked and counted. When the count had been verified by all the tellers, the ballots were burned and the ashes dumped into the street sewer at the corner of the church lot. I thanked him for calling and hung up. Then I calmly gave my family the news. One or two were surprised, but there were no tears, no angry outbursts, only a quiet acceptance of the facts. I can never forget, nor will I ever cease to be grateful for, the support of my wife and children at that time. Grace and I knew we had the respect and love of our children, and that was worth more than anything else in the world to us.

At the evening service the chairman of the deacons made the official announcement to the congregation, about one-fourth the size of the morning crowd, but everybody knew already. There were reporters present who aired the results on radio, television, and in the local papers. The national press services picked up the news, and it became world-wide information.

After the chairman's report to the congregation, I made a statement that evidently was not understood at all. I spoke of the Baptist democratic process, of the rule of the majority, and expressed the hope that the congregation would not allow the difference of opinion to destroy the effective working of the church. I did not scold the congregation for its vote and avoided either giving any comfort to the victors or commiserating with the losers. My disappointment in the vote was carefully covered, and I made no prophecies of the future. I knew there were segregationists who respected me and wanted me to continue as pastor.

The next day we notified the authorities at Mercer of the action of the church. We asked them to inform the Negroes on campus of the situation. We sent a plea to the Negro leaders of Macon that there be no demonstrations and expressed the hope that none of their people would be embarrassed by being turned away from our church. This was one of the most humiliating actions of my entire life, for I had been dedicated to influencing people to attend God's house and associate themselves with Christ's church. I had determined that I would abide by the decision of the congregation to the "letter of the law" in all my official responsibilities. This I did.

The Mercer officials were most understanding and helpful.

One of them, a close friend, spared me the personal embarrassment of communicating with the Negro leaders of Macon. Their response was a tribute both to Mercer and to the black community. Not one word of criticism or recrimination came from these two sources. Their understanding of our struggle was a source of comfort to me and others among us.

Early on Monday I received a painful call from a Negro teacher who was attending summer school at Mercer. He was very polite, but forthright in his expression of intent. "Your church voted yesterday to close its doors to Negroes — is that correct?" he asked. I answered, "Yes, it is correct." He then said, "I would like to suggest that you come to the Mercer Student Center and remove the signs that are there inviting people to your worship services, or you should state that the invitation is to whites only."

There was no adequate answer for his rebuke. His reaction was reasonable. The university had admitted him, but the church on the university campus would not allow him to worship God there. He might not want to come to our church. I doubted that he did. But his sense of human dignity was outraged by the fact that if he did desire to, he would be forbidden because of the color of his skin. I apologized for the action of my church and told him that it was in opposition to everything I believed and preached.

Reporters telephoned on Monday, July 25, asking for statements for the press. I made no comment at that time, hoping not to add to our humiliation and embarrassment by a public airing of the controversy. After all, honesty would force me to publicly repudiate the action of my people. But it was humanly impossible to prevent a public response to the church's action. Letters began to come to me and to the chairman of the deacons condemning us for our vote. In the absence of a public statement of my personal views, I was classified, among those who did not know me, as a segregationist, approving of what the church had done. A number of letter writers blamed me for leading my congregation to close its doors to Negroes.

It is impossible to express the frustration that arose over my personal dilemma. I wanted to lead all my people, but could not do so if I took sides in the news media. To project myself as a symbol of controversy was furthest from my desires. I persisted in the vain hope that there could be a reversal of majority sentiment at a later time.

I suppose I was the naive product of a form of ministerial training predicated on the spurious belief that a pastor has failed if he allows his congregation to be divided over a controversial issue. He must keep peace at any price, and if that peace is impossible, he must save the congregation as much embarrassment as possible even to the sacrificing of himself.

Until then in my ministerial career I had been successful as a peacemaker and leader of divided congregations. I had never before been thrust into a situation where it was necessary to oppose congregational leaders on a great moral issue. My integrity as a Christian was involved and I could not avoid the issue, but in such circumstances one can do nothing "right" so far as official acts are concerned. Since one's position is judged to be wrong, any action taken in the implementation of it is *ipso facto* wrong. This is the essence of the great agony that comes to any person who is loyal to ideals that will not be accepted by the majority.

In the eyes of many I was identified as the pastor of a church that had violated Christian principles, and as long as I remained the pastor of that church that identity remained. What must I do? Resign and disassociate myself from this identity or remain and continue in the controversy? I chose to remain. That choice forced a further intensification of the unpleasantness. The congregation had to endure a minister who felt conscience-bound to maintain a position in direct opposition to the views of the majority.

Should I preach sermons on the issue? I did, because I was in the midst of the series of sermons on the book of Acts which had been launched earlier. By mid-July my sermon topics were from the heart of the book, and the race issue was implied in every chapter. This issue, involving Gentiles, was the first great controversy that claimed the young church's attention. It divided the congregation at Jerusalem permanently. Why persist in preaching on such a sensitive subject when all advice was to talk about matters far removed and let the people rest awhile? It would have been an act of cowardice to turn from my advertised course. Furthermore, my sense of personal involvement was too strong to do so. As I see the biblical doctrine of man, it is universal in all its parts. There is no such thing as a "race issue," but the "human race issue." I decided to go full speed ahead, regardless of the backlash, for this was my personal Gethsemane. I could not be true to my commitment to Christ and do otherwise.

Practical pastors and "hardheaded" laymen have called my course foolish. They were not with me when a deacon came and said, "Tom, you can solve this problem if you want to. Our people don't want you to leave. You can bring our church together if you will preach just one sermon. Just one sermon will do the trick."

"What would that sermon be?" I asked.

"I don't have to tell you. You know," he answered.

Yes, I knew what it would be — an admission of error in my basic position and a public statement that I had erred. This would end the confrontation and probably relieve most of the tension. This would "save the church." Perhaps I would then be considered a wise administrator by many of my fellow pastors and denominational leaders. But, having done that, the only course left to me would be the preaching of bland sermons and the avoidance of any attempt to develop a relevant ministry. This would simply be a marking of time. For who can follow a minister who has denied his conscience, lost his self-respect, and ultimately will lose the respect of his friends and enemies?

9

SENSING MY DILEMMA, Editor John Hurt called me from Atlanta Tuesday morning to ask about recent developments. I told him that we were getting letters almost daily and that some of them were accusing me of promoting the "closed-doors" vote. He asked me to give him a statement for *The Christian Index*. I told him that I should make no statements at that time. He disagreed and asked me to come to Atlanta and discuss my future course of action with him.

I told Grace about John's call. She agreed with him that I should make a statement disassociating myself from the action of the church. She viewed my discharge as inevitable and had resigned herself to it. The only hope that she saw for the church to realize its potential was for a large number of segregationists, including those of the power structure, to leave and join other churches. I believed they would never do so. It was "their" church. They were in power. They had just won a resounding victory in closing the doors to black people. All they had to do was wait and their ministers would be gone, and their problems would be solved.

On Thursday morning Grace and I drove to Atlanta to see John Hurt. I spent two hours in his office with him and

Jack Harwell, associate editor, who later succeeded him when he accepted the editorship of the *Baptist Standard* in Texas. At first Hurt probed me with searching questions to get the full picture. His conclusion was that I could not stay at Tattnall Square regardless of what I said and did from this point on, and that I should now concentrate on making my position on the race issue unmistakably clear. He began to urge me to make a statement for publication that would touch the consciences of Georgia Baptists.

The summer of 1966 found the state locked in a gubernatorial primary election campaign that boiled down to a fight between former Governor Ellis Arnall and Lester Maddox. Arnall, who published his credo in a book entitled *The Shore Dimly Seen,* won national fame as a liberal governor in the Talmadge era of the 40's. The image of Lester Maddox is well known. This was the historical and psychological setting of our controversy.

It is difficult for the average American to realize how strong the southern racial mystique is. It has been nurtured for more than 150 years. It is as deeply ingrained in southerners as their basic Protestant character. As a matter of fact, the two have become so intertwined in southern minds and hearts that an attack on one produces a Pavlovian response from the other. In Georgia, where politics is always a major interest, especially with its racial overtones, the reasoned approach is scorned and candidates are forced to deal almost exclusively with the so-called "gut issue." It is foolhardy for a southern minister to believe that a great many of his church leaders are going to take any action that appears "unpatriotic" to the southern mind or "communist inspired" during a political campaign.

I knew all this, but being an optimist, I would not easily accept the fact. John Hurt led me to do this. He insisted that I had done my duty in my church, that I had offered myself as a sacrifice which would surely be accepted. He felt that I now owed it to myself, my denomination, and my region, to make as great a witness as possible. Still I shrank from any action that would intensify the suffering of my family and my supporters in the church. It was painfully evident that the church power structure had launched a campaign to make life miserable for those who voted for an "open door." I had never had the occasion before to witness the sometimes subtle, sometimes naked, attacks that some "Christians" are able to make on one another in a bitter controversy. It was distressing to observe the hatred manifested in the lives of those who were nominally committed to follow the One who said, "A new commandment I give to you, that you love one another; even as I have loved you" (RSV).

When I persisted in my "no statement" policy, Hurt arose from his desk, walked around, and looked me straight in the eye. "All right, Holmes," he asked bluntly, "what do you want to be — the voice of a prophet, or the chant of a priest?"

That was the clincher. I replied, "Give me a sheet of paper." Instead, John Hurt sat down at his typewriter and did the actual drafting of what I wanted to say. The finished statement read: "I have not and cannot be a party to closing our church doors to any person wanting to enter and worship. A pastor's heart may be broken by a church action, but, for a time at least, he has a pastor's responsibility to his membership. I must say no more at the present."

After leaving Hurt's office, Grace and I decided to visit Mr. Eugene Patterson, editor of *The Atlanta Constitution*. Hurt had done more than he realized when he led me to see that the matter would eventually burst into wide publicity. I wanted the papers to say nothing for as long as possible, but I wanted them to have all the contributing facts at hand when the final events occurred.

Mr. Patterson was familiar with the news. He listened most sympathetically for an hour as we gave him the whole background of the controversy. We also left with him an outline of events up to that date which Douglas Johnson and I had prepared and mailed to a number of interested parties.

I was concerned that the truth be known about the relationship of the Mercer officers to the controversy. One story had it that President Harris was directing me in every move I made. It was whispered that he had integrated Mercer and Vineville Baptist Church and was now taking on Tattnall Square. The accusations notwithstanding, President Harris and other university officers had carefully avoided any participation whatsoever in the affair. I had only one conversation with President Harris from June until late September and that was about a prospective gift for the new Science Center.

When members of Tattnall Square received the August 4 issue of *The Christian Index* containing my statement, the "fat was really in the fire." At prayer meeting on Wednesday night, the faces of the opposing deacons and their wives mirrored unmistakably their fierce anger. Strange as it may seem, however, not a one spoke out against me. I suppose they had decided it was now useless.

One morning soon afterward, I received a telephone call from a woman member of the church. She said, "Pastor, I have just learned something that I think you ought to know. Two of our deacons are Klansmen." When she named one man, I was not surprised. He was the kind of insecure person who likes to join every organization in existence if it can in any way bolster his ego. He was easily led by others with more powerful personalities. This news just confirmed the suspicions I had. She did not name the other person and I did not ask her to, but I was certain I knew the man.

On Saturday morning, August 13, I was in my study at the church finishing my preparations to preach on Sunday. There was a knock at my door. It was a minister friend. He told me that he was a personal friend of two of the FBI agents in the city. One of them had called him and asked him to warn me of rumors that the Klansmen were talking about some sort of demonstration against Douglas Johnson and me. They could not say what it was or when it would occur, but I was to be on my guard.

I was not surprised at the Klan's interest. They were

strong in the Macon area, and I had made several comments about the Klan in my morning sermons which were broadcast over WNEX radio in Macon. This was not the first time in my life that I had been warned of possible violence at the hands of the hooded night riders. Without boasting, I was not frightened by this warning. I have always felt that most Klansmen are basically cowards. Their operations are aimed at intimidation and usually are against helpless people, or those they believe will have no way to fight back.

If two of the deacons were Klansmen, I felt they would see to it that the parsonage was not bombed, because it was owned by the church. However, I considered cross burning on our front lawn a possibility. No demonstrations materialized, but I did receive vile, anonymous letters, which I attributed to Klansmen or Klan types.

As it turned out, a Klan lynching was not in the cards for the ministers of Tattnall Square Baptist Church. Rather this was to be a "due process" execution by fellow officers and members of the church.

10

NOBODY BUT A PASTOR can understand the feeling of drained
weariness that characterizes Monday for pastors. For that
reason, I never did like to have any important meetings on
Monday night, but the convenience of the lay members has
to be considered, and in my pastorates the deacons almost
always chose to meet that night.

I very often was not at my best at those meetings. This was
especially true on Monday night, August 15, when I made
my way to the drab classroom in the educational building
for the monthly deacons' meeting at Tattnall Square. The
hostility I saw all about me only added to the strain that I
was feeling night and day. Doug's face was drawn and tired.

I shook hands with every man in the room, knowing that
some preferred not to. I had determined to maintain as
gracious an attitude as possible in spite of anything to the
contrary, expressed or unexpressed. It was evident that this
meeting was to be a very ugly one because of the warning
received on Saturday and a phone call from a friend in
Columbus, Georgia. I will say more about that later.

I had had another call that day, from our head usher, an ex-
treme segregationist. He had openly expressed to me his

opposition to my views, but he had carried out to the letter the instructions of the deacon chairman when the Negro students came on June 29. Apparently, many had condemned him for seating the Negroes. He had explained why he did so. Now he was angry. He said, "The chairman of the deacons is telling everybody that he didn't tell me to seat the niggers. You know that's a lie." I told him that it was indeed a falsehood if the chairman had denied telling him so because I had overheard the conversation when the chairman had instructed him, and through him, the ushers. Also the chairman himself had told me of the conversation.

I considered it strange that the head usher would call me to tell me this, because it only revealed that our chairman, good man that he was, had yielded to pressures from the controlling clique. He had joined them in their contention that the pastor had pulled a fast one on the church and had timed it when the chairman was out of town. I told the head usher that since he would be at the deacons' meeting that night he could set the record straight and I would certainly support him in it.

The meeting was opened with a devotional as usual, and the minutes were read and approved. The chairman then addressed the group. He said, "Brethren, I am six feet, four inches tall, and I weigh 265 pounds. I want you to know that I am well able to see to it that we have order here tonight." This was the first time in my life I had ever heard a deacon open a meeting with such a declaration. I couldn't understand to whom this warning was directed. However, he knew that a storm was about to break and it did that minute.

A deacon who had been in office less than a year asked for and got the floor. He charged that I was continuing to agitate the race issue in every sermon I preached and that matters were going from bad to worse. He moved that the deacons recommend to the church that, "Tom, Doug, and Jack be asked to resign." His motion was seconded immediately.

This was the first time in my ministerial career that such

a motion had ever been made regarding me. It was no surprise on this occasion, however, and I had no unusual emotional reaction except a feeling of curiosity about how they would accomplish this execution. Another deacon suggested that Doug and I might wish to retire from the meeting. Perhaps I should have left, but I decided to stay for awhile at least. I said with some asperity, "Brother Chairman, if these brethren can stand to say what they plan to say, I think we can stand to listen to it."

I knew some of the things that would probably be said. My friend in Columbus had reported that he had heard a rumor that the pastor was stealing money from the church. From this I had deduced that someone had it in mind to accuse me of stealing from the benevolent or poor fund. This was the only church money that I had ever handled. This fund was administered through a special checking account by a committee of three — the financial secretary, another member who was the head usher, and myself. Either the other member or I had to countersign checks drawn on this fund by the secretary. On several occasions when the other member was not available for meetings, the financial secretary and I had issued checks for food and other aid, and I had delivered it in my car.

After my friend told me of this misleading rumor, I went to the financial secretary and asked her to prepare a listing of every check issued on the account, with the date, and to whom the assistance went. I had this record in my pocket to use if the matter came up. The financial secretary was working with D. K. reporting on everything I did, every visitor I had at my study, and every request I made at the office. She was not a malicious woman and I know this was all very distasteful to her, but she was at the chief deacon's mercy. She was past sixty years old and needed the work; she could hold her job only by doing as the chief demanded. Doubtless, she had warned him of my preparation for a counterattack at the deacons' meeting.

Sure enough, the head usher arose and with a written

speech began his attack. At the very first intimation that he was going to accuse me of misappropriation of funds, the chairman called him out of order and told him to be seated. The chairman knew that I had the facts to refute the accusation and thus weaken their attack. He also knew of the head usher's intention of setting the record straight on the chairman's instructions on seating the Negroes. The chairman definitely did not want this out in the open, as it would have precipitated a fight among the opposing deacons.

Albert Harris, the first deacon to call me and pledge his support when the controversy began, arose and began to defend the three of us. He pointed out that the church had dishonored itself in voting to close its doors to Negroes, and would add more shame if we were discharged for trying to give Christian leadership in the racial controversy. He told the deacons that their efforts to manufacture other charges against us were a defensive action to cover up their unchristian attitudes.

Albert had a hearing problem and wore a hearing aid. All the time he was speaking, Rayford Brown was sitting in a chair directly in front of him heckling him unmercifully. (This was the man, whose real name I am not using, who accosted me the night after the Negro visitors came to church.) As Albert would make each statement, Rayford would shout at him, "Louder, louder. We can't hear you." This mockery was the cruelest act I had ever witnessed in a Christian gathering. The chairman did nothing about this heckling for some time. He finally called for order, and Brown moved to a chair on the back row. Albert was patient and in the most gracious manner possible finished his speech. His conduct to the bitter end was that of a gentleman.

When Albert resumed his seat, D. K. took the floor. He talked about Baptist polity, that the majority rules, etc. He accused me of breaking my word to the congregation, referring to the public statement I had made the night following the vote to close the doors. The gist of his talk was that I should make my preaching fit the policy of the congregation.

At this point I decided that a reply was essential on my part. The issue was no longer restricted to race. The chief deacon had broadened it to include the freedom of the pulpit. With this fundamental issue now clearly in the open, I could no longer be silent. I asked for the floor. When I began to speak, I was heckled by Brown and interrupted twice by D. K. I was angry by this time, more so than I had ever been in any church meeting before. I bluntly told D. K. to keep quiet. He had had his say with no interruptions, and now I intended to have mine. I stood for fully a minute staring into his face, daring him to interrupt me again.

I then defended my preaching and my actions, with the following points. One, I had respected the closed-door policy fully in actions stated earlier. I had seen to it that no Negroes came to the church again. Two, I was following my announced preaching program and was preaching on the "human race" issue as it is presented in the book of Acts. Three, the church could vote any policy it desired, but it could not bind my conscience by its vote. "My conscience belongs to God, and a thousand votes by the church would not bind it," I asserted.

I declared that the pulpit must be free for the man of God to speak the Word of God as it is revealed to him. I declared that the person in the pew is also free to accept or reject the preacher and his message. I concluded by saying: "This church called me to preach the Word of God. The vote was unanimous, which means that you men here tonight also voted for me. Your action, however, places me in the position where I must insist that the church decide whether it accepts or rejects me and the message I preach. I will not resign. You must take this matter to the church."

With that I excused myself and asked Doug to leave the meeting with me. With a strange feeling of relief, Doug and I walked out into the hot August night. We found ourselves walking toward the Mercer Student Center.

I called Grace, told her of the motion then before the deacons, and said I was certain it would pass. Her only answer was, "Rejoice and be glad!" I knew she was thinking of Matthew 5:12, "Rejoice, and be exceeding glad: for great is your reward in heaven: for so persecuted they the prophets which were before you" — and I was encouraged.

Then Doug and I walked into the student snack bar and ordered Cokes. We sat down to "cool off" and talk for a bit.

Doug had been approached by the officials of another university with a tentative offer to become director of religious activities. Knowing what must happen if he remained at Tattnall Square, I advised him to accept the offer if it became firm. He was young, with a wife and four small children, and he stood to lose much more than either Jack Jones or I. But Doug is a young man of integrity. He doggedly refused to resign and leave the fight, though time has proven that it cost him more than any of us. I can never forget such devotion to duty.

After finishing our break, Doug and I went to our homes. I cannot remember my thoughts as I drove home. It seems to me now that I was so numb with fatigue and disappointment that my memory fails me. Some time after my return home, Grace and I were seated in the living room. The doorbell rang. There at the door were three young deacons, who had come to tell me that the vote was twelve to nine in favor of our discharge. Heroically, they had done what they could to prevent the passing of the motion. They were near tears. I do remember accepting the news quietly with no comments. After a few minutes I asked these deacons to pray with me. I prayed that we all would have strength for whatever we had to face and that some good somehow might come.

In a few minutes we had additional visitors. They were Annette Highsmith and Miss Leone Bates, one of the Mercer faculty who was a member of Tattnall Square Church. They were in tears and had come to bring comfort to Grace and me. Grace took them into the guest bedroom where they talked for a while. When they came out, Annette and Miss Bates were smiling. They said, "We came to comfort Grace, but she has comforted us." They left, and we went to bed.

We slept from sheer exhaustion. The next morning we were up early, Grace drinking her coffee and reading her Bible on the side porch, where she had a view of the lovely little creek and woods to the rear of the house. After I had done my morning exercises, I sat by the picture window to watch for the pair of quail that came out of the woods to the bird feeder on the back lawn each morning and evening. They were beautiful birds, and we had named them Faith and Hope. They seemed to be a tie that bound us to the beauty and order of God's world untouched by man's inhumanity to man. Without faith, hope — and love — what is there for mankind in this world?

By now Grace and I were feeling the strain of this controversy very heavily. We decided that we must take a vacation. Following a suggestion of our friend and my teacher, Dr. Edward McDowell, we rented a cottage for two weeks at Holden Beach, North Carolina. Our daughter and her husband were to join us there, driving from Nashville. However, our preparation for departure was interrupted many times by friends calling to express their regret at the action of the deacons. Some of these decided to try to force an immediate vote on the action of the deacons at the conference on Wednesday night. They began to call our supporters in the church membership and ask them to be present for the conference, prepared to take a stand.

Words of the deacons' action and the anticipated showdown in the congregation leaked to the press. So when the conference began at the church on Wednesday night Dick Hebert of *The Atlanta Constitution* and reporters from the Macon newspapers were there. I didn't know any of them at the time, but they were spotted by men of the church. So as soon as the usual hymn, devotional, and prayer were finished, a member of the church asked if we didn't have members of the press present. I repeated the question, asking any reporters present to please rise. When they did so, a motion was made that they be excluded from the conference, and it was passed.

More than two hundred people were in attendance, the largest number I had ever seen at a regular business meeting of the church. In the routine order of business we came to the report of the board of deacons. When I called for this report, the chairman arose to say that the deacons had no report for the conference. There was not a person in the room who didn't know what had happened in the deacons' meeting; so the chairman's statement was entirely unsatisfactory, especially to our supporters.

One of the members, not a deacon, asked to speak. He asserted that the actions of the deacons were always matters of concern to the congregation. He said he had heard a report that the deacons had requested the resignation of the pastor, the associate pastor, and the minister of music. He declared that this matter should be brought before the congregation, and he concluded by making a motion to that effect. Several people seconded the motion.

There followed a lengthy discussion of the action of the deacons, with the pastor as moderator. Following my usual procedure, I presided in an informal and open manner allowing everyone to express himself freely. Dr. Harold McManus, chairman of the Department of Christianity at Mercer University and a longtime member of the church, asked for the floor. In a prepared statement he charged that for years the deacons had run the church without proper reporting of their actions to the congregation. He said they had, in effect, usurped the autonomy of the congregation.

This forthright statement infuriated the deacons who had voted for our resignations. The chairman of the finance committee came forward as one of their spokesmen. First, he indicted my leadership by presenting a negative picture of church offerings, Sunday school attendance, etc. He then accused me of betraying the church. He said that in the deacons' meeting in July, R. J. had stated that I had promised him that Negroes would never be allowed at our church, and that this matter would never be a source of trouble to the congregation. He said that when R. J. had made this statement in the deacons' meeting the pastor did not deny it. Therefore, he and the other deacons had concluded that the statement was true.

Interrupting him, I stated that the reason I hadn't replied to R. J.'s statement was that it would be necessary to call him a liar, and I had not wanted to do that. However, I was in effect calling him a liar then. He was present at this meeting and a gasp came from the audience. Many were shocked by my daring to impugn the word of the wealthiest man, the largest contributor, and one of the oldest and most devoted leaders of the congregation. The agony of this whole controversy seemed to reach a crux at this point in my own emotions. R. J. and I had been close friends. We had been golf partners and he had shown me many kindnesses. However, the patent effort to cast me in the role of grand deceiver had to be met head-on. I called upon the members of the pulpit committee and the board of deacons who were present to bear witness that before my call to this pastorate all my conversations regarding the worship of Negroes in the church were the very opposite of his claim.

This exchange heated things up considerably. The conference became even more tense as a number of young people came forward and condemned the action of the deacons. They made pleas for the church to open its doors to all people and truly present a Christian witness on the campus and in the community.

After a very large number of people had spoken, the deacon chairman came forward to make his first public statement in the controversy. He accused me of waiting until he was on an out-of-state trip to bring the Negroes to the worship services. He said the pastor wanted to destroy the church, basing his charge on preliminary talks that I had had with two leaders of First Baptist Church about a possible merger of their congregation and ours for a more effective inner-city witness.

This discussion had now run about two hours and was getting increasingly bitter, so someone called for a vote on the main question; namely, that the deacons' recommendation concerning the three ministers be presented for immediate action. The motion lost by four votes.

Dr. Spencer B. King, Jr., professor of history at Mercer, was preparing a history of the church for its 75th Anniversary celebration September 11. He made a motion that the celebration be postponed and the church act on the recommendation of the deacons on September 25. Dr. King was hopeful that a delay might bring a change in the views of the congregation. This motion was passed.

Feeling was then so intense that a woman fainted. At my suggestion, the conference was adjourned, and we went out into the sultry night.

The reporters were still present. By interviewing a number of people they got the story, and it was prominently displayed in the newspapers the next morning.

I learned that Dick Hebert was using the phone in the Mercer News Bureau to call his story to Atlanta. I went there, made his acquaintance, and apologized for the treatment he had received.

Grace and I had just finished breakfast that Thursday morning when the phone rang. The Associated Press was on the line. I was asked for a comment on the controversy and I stated, "I have just tried in my ministry to make the Christian faith relevant to our modern world. I cannot agree to close the doors of my church to anyone who desires to worship God."

As soon as Grace and I could arrange to do so, we packed our bags and departed from Macon for Holden Beach, North Carolina, to meet my daughter and her husband and Dr. and Mrs. McDowell and their family for a few days of rest. Doug Johnson preached on the two Sundays we were away.

Grace and I love the ocean. In a little cabin by the sea at Holden Beach we tried to unwind from the tremendous tensions that had been building within us. We were unable, however, to get away from the trouble at Tattnall Square, where the siege was continuing.

11

AT OUR SEASIDE RETREAT we received long distance calls from friends in various cities who were reacting to the news of the church dispute and our threatened dismissal. Calls also came from strangers across the country.

John Hurt mailed a marked copy of *The Christian Index* for August 25 containing his editorial on our struggle. Entitled "Tattnall Decision Affects Many," it read:

No Baptist church is an island unto itself. Each is sovereign, to be sure, with supreme allegiance to God. There also is a responsibility to others which cannot be ignored.

So it is now with the Tattnall Square Baptist Church in Macon. Its location on the edge of Mercer University's campus gives it a status far greater than for most churches its size.

The church is embroiled in controversy over the seating of Negroes. The cameras of world opinion are focused there. Nothing the church can do will alter that fact.

Discharge of Thomas J. Holmes and his staff, recommended by a majority of deacons, is not the issue. His reputation through the years is too well established for the stain, if imposed, to be other than a badge of honor.

The real issue at Tattnall Square Baptist Church is the future of that one church—and whether there will be another burden for those who seek to win a lost world to Christ.

This editorial brought strength to Grace and me. We shall ever be grateful to John Hurt for the support that he gave us. Other Baptist state paper editors were championing our cause, notably Dr. Erwin L. McDonald, *Arkansas Baptist Newsmagazine;* Dr. C. R. Daley, *Western Recorder* (Kentucky); and Mr. J. Marse Grant, *Biblical Recorder* (North Carolina).

After a week of surf bathing and fishing, we left Holden Beach on August 26 and returned over the weekend to Macon. When we arrived there, we discovered that many wild rumors were being broadcast around the city. The Macon papers had editorialized about the controversy, and it was being said that I had written the editorials. It had also been stated that Grace and I had gone to California where there were a number of student demonstrations and marches for civil rights and that we had joined the marches there. Another wild rumor was that President Harris was dictating my every move at the church. It was being said that the NAACP had given us ten thousand dollars to integrate the congregation. According to this story, President Harris had received five thousand dollars and I had received the other five thousand.

Following my policy I decided to make no public replies to these ridiculous rumors. I did let it be known that I would be glad to set the record straight with anyone who would come directly to me with these tales, and several individuals accepted my offer. It was then that I noticed that our support was growing among the members of the church. They were beginning to see that D. K., R. J., and their hard-core supporters were really using this controversy in an effort to get rid of the ministers.

I continued to preach from the book of Acts, letting the chips fall where they would as I expounded on the tremendous incidents in the history of the early church. The relevance of this book was simply amazing. Its truths cut two ways: on the one hand, they infuriated my adversaries in the church; on the other hand, they gave real spiritual guidance to those people who were seeking to discover the mind of Christ.

It was about this time that Doug Johnson informed me in the study one day that a number of summer school students were trying to find ways to help us. They were receiving letters from other students who would be returning to the university campus on about September 15 for the fall quarter. They wanted to start a movement to get perhaps two hundred students to join the church on September 18 so that they could vote the next Sunday on the deacons' recommendation demanding our resignation.

I heard some of the deacons were afraid this might be done and were going to offer a resolution to restrict the voting to persons who had been members of the church at least six months. Such action on their part was unnecessary, however, because I asked Doug to advise the student leaders that I could not favor their planned maneuver. We felt it would not accomplish the real purpose of our stand — which was to lead the congregation to make a decision that would vitally affect their future. We could have brought into the church enough students to have won a majority vote, but that was not the kind of victory we sought.

At the same time I was receiving letters and telegrams from aroused churchmen across the country and from missionaries abroad. These communications were 98 percent in support of our position, and they assured us of prayers and concern. Some of our friends mimeographed letters to the church membership in which they pled with the people to reject the leadership of the chief deacon and his clique and to sustain our ministry, but to no avail.

Dr. W. G. Lee, who was going strong at ninety-three when this was written, a great Christian, and one of the best friends I ever had, was often in my home giving counsel and support through the awful days of this controversy. He has been active in every good movement in Macon in the last sixty years. He had been particularly prominent in the promotion of the Dudley Hughes Vocational School in Macon.

One day he asked me to visit Mr. Raymonde Kelley, the director of the school, and see what was going on in the beautiful new building on Forsyth Street.

When we went, Mr. Kelley showed us around the various classrooms, offices, and laboratories. The director told us about one of the very fine instructors in the school who was a Negro officer from Warner Robins Center. His class was in session at the time and we went into the room to listen to a part of his lecture. I saw black and white youths seated side by side and learning together in a secular institution.

As I observed this demonstration of orderly adjustment to social change in the secular realm, I was overwhelmed by the irony of backwardness and reaction in the church of Jesus Christ. Whites and blacks could learn a trade together, read books side by side in the public library, play ball together, go to the movies together — but they could not enter the house of God and worship their Maker together!

The tragic paradox of the situation came to me with such visceral force that I was overcome. Excusing myself, I went into a vacant room on the hall and closed the door. There I broke down and wept bitter tears over the destructive influence of the segregationists in the life of the church. I could see the failures of the people of God in not giving leadership to society in a time of crisis. Turning to prayer, I literally begged the Lord to give us the victory that we might reverse the situation in our city.

I do not know how long I was there. Finally, I was able to get control of myself and return to the hall where Mr. Kelley and Dr. Lee were waiting for me. They knew what had happened. They were very sympathetic. I realized how near to collapse I was at that time because very seldom in my life have I reached the point where I lost control of my emotions. It was a bit frightening.

The unrelenting pressure of our adversaries was beginning to get to me. Their strategy was to delay the final vote as long as possible in the hope that the harassment and suspense would force Doug Johnson, Jack Jones, and me to resign.

My physician advised me to resign and get out of the controversy because he felt I was now under too much strain to continue.

Jack returned from New York, where he had been doing graduate study at Union Theological Seminary. He, Doug, and I met to discuss what our course of action should be. We concluded that we would go on as if nothing had happened — ministering to the people, doing our respective duties, making no difference between friend and foe — and we would not resign.

The pressure naturally caused us to reconsider and to discuss resigning several times as we thought about our friends and families. Each time we decided that quitting was impossible. So by the grace of God we were given strength to continue our work.

As the regular September church conference approached, I did make certain concessions that were very difficult for me. I decided I should not attempt to preside at the congregational meeting set for September 21 due to my physical condition and so informed the chairman of the deacons. I also avoided the deacons' meeting of the 19th. The Rev. Robert L. O'Brien, associational missionary, was asked to serve as moderator of the church conference in my stead.

The report of the nominating committee for the officers for the church year, 1966-67, was supposed to have been made in the August conference, but when the meeting was adjourned at the end of the long controversial session, this report had not been made. My supporters had decided that nothing could be done to rescue the church from its downhill plunge unless the leadership was in more just and reasonable hands. So they decided to make a last-ditch effort to change the leadership. On Saturday afternoon, September 17, a leading member called a meeting in his office of a number of men of the church sympathetic to us. He invited me to be present. After spending a time in prayer, they drew up a slate of new church officers and decided on a strategy of seeking to substitute this slate for the regular report of the nominating committee. If successful, they felt they could save our ministry and restore progress in the church.

The test came on the night of September 21, but D. K., R. J., and their associates "got out the vote," and every effort of our followers to change the leadership of the church was defeated.

It was clear then that the battle was lost. All we could do was to await September 25 and the final vote.

12

Beginning on Sunday, September 11, we had a week of study for the expansion of the Sunday school, which was directed by Dr. Julian Pipkin, secretary of the Department of Sunday School work of the Georgia Baptist Convention. Dr. Pipkin preached on Sunday morning, September 11, and I did not attend the service. Being practically exhausted, I stayed at home in bed. Each night during the week following I was able to meet at the church for the study periods with the faithful workers of the Sunday school.

Dr. Pipkin did the best he could to ignore the controversy and concentrate upon the task at hand, which was an effort to reach the people of our community for Bible study and church membership. We were struck by the fact that the real leadership of the church, other than the dissident deacons, was with us. They came each night, studied, talked, and prayed together about the work and the mission of the church.

The week following was uneventful except for the regular monthly conference which I have reported in the preceding chapter.

Sunday morning, September 25, was a beautiful morning

and we made our way to the church at a few minutes before eleven. I had earlier considered various subjects that I might use that morning, had settled on "My Impossible Dream," and had broken ground for a sermon on that subject. It would be a review of my original objectives when I came as pastor, what we had tried to do to realize the dream, and the events that had shattered it.

However, Doug Johnson and I decided that I should not preach. Rather, we would let other people speak concerning the issues as they saw them and how the action of the church would affect the worldwide missions program of Southern Baptists and other American Christians. He would read a letter which he had received from a classmate at Mercer who was now a minister of a church in Florida. I would read two letters from missionaries who had been members of the Tattnall Square Church when they had been students at Mercer.

When we went into the pulpit at two or three minutes before eleven, the house was filled. All available chairs had been placed in the aisles. A number of students were present. Conspicuous among them was a Chinese youth whose family had fled the Communists in China. He was a graduate student at Mercer. Reared as a Buddhist, he had been deeply interested in becoming a Christian, but his mind had been confused by the controversy at Tattnall Square. I had talked with him privately a number of times about making a public profession of faith. At one time I was certain that he would do so, but after he saw what happened at the campus church that day, he turned away from Christianity. I had talked with him about it one more time several months later, and he showed no interest whatsoever in becoming a Christian.

Accompanying this young Oriental that morning was a student from the Middle East whose skin was so dark that he was almost mistaken for a Negro and excluded from the service. The ushers finally decided that he was not a Negro and admitted him.

Unknown to me at the time, Sam Oni, the African student,

appeared at one of the two main entrances of the church and tried to get in to express to me or to the deacons his great concern over what he had heard and observed of the events at Tattnall Square. As related in Chapter One, he was forcibly prevented from doing so.

After the singing of the great hymn, "Where Cross the Crowded Ways of Life," and after other parts of the worship service were concluded, Doug read the letter from his pastor friend, and I read the two letters from the missionaries. As we expected, the minds of those who were opposed to us were closed, and no plea from any quarter could reach them; so none was attempted. I made the statement that the church would be called into conference and that the chairman of the deacons would preside. Then Grace and I, Doug and his family, and Jack Jones left the building.

As Grace and I drove home, we turned on the radio to the station that regularly broadcasts our service and heard Mrs. John Harrison, the widow of a former pastor, making a speech to the congregation. She pled with the people not to destroy the life and ministry of the church by our discharge. Although I did not hear any more of the broadcast, I understand that after she had finished, another woman member spoke in rebuttal. She argued that the real issue was not race but the leadership of the ministers of the church. It was our failure, she maintained, that forced the deacons to take the actions and make the recommendations which were now before the congregation.

I don't know all that transpired. I understand that after these two speeches were finished, the vote was taken.

At about 2:30 in the afternoon, I received a telephone call from the superintendent of the Sunday school stating that the votes had been counted and that the church had voted that we resign. I called Doug Johnson and Jack Jones. They came to my home, went into the study downstairs, and there we composed a statement that was issued jointly to the press, as follows:

"We can feel only sorrow at this action of the Tattnall

Square Baptist Church in discharging us from our positions. Not sorrow for ourselves, but sorrow that a church with such a distinguished history of Christian service and with such a great opportunity for the future has allowed itself to be shattered over the issue of the seating of all persons who desire to worship in our sanctuary. This church is blessed with many fine Christians. It is our hope that these people will now devote their energies toward rebuilding the church.

"The privilege of working together as ministers to the church has been a stimulating experience. We are grateful for the cordial and friendly relations we have had with many of the people. Our continued prayers will be directed to the strengthening of this church in its future work."

The three of us signed this statement. Representatives of the newspapers and of radio and television came to my home. I read the statement, and it was immediately broadcast to the community.

Doug, Jack, and I then discussed what we would do about submitting our resignations at the evening service. None of us wished to prolong our embarrassment or that of our supporters. We decided that we would merely go to the church, read our resignations, and go home. However, at about that time the phone rang. It was the superintendent of the Sunday school, calling to tell me that he had been in a conference with a number of the people of the church. They had been talking and praying, and they wanted to ask me to preach one more time from that pulpit. I told him how weary I was and how this rejection had affected us all, and that we would rather not conduct a regular service. At their continued insistence, we agreed to have a worship service, and I agreed to preach.

Doug and Jack went to their homes to prepare for the evening service. I spent some time in meditation and in prayer trying to prepare myself to preach. The text that came to me was from Isaiah 55, "Seek ye the Lord while he may be found, call ye upon him while he is near." My subject was "An Invitation We Cannot Afford to Decline."

We went to the church, and somehow I was strangely buoyed by the spirit of God and found strength to preach one of the most satisfying sermons that I've ever delivered. I talked about the continuous nearness of God and how his nearness is manifested to us. I then spoke of God's constant willingness to share with us in the everyday needs of our lives. I was speaking primarily, of course, to our heart-broken friends and making a plea to them to lean heavily upon God and to seek his wisdom and his grace at this time. It was also a testimony of how I had felt the nearness of the Father during all of these tragic weeks and months. Never in my life had I known the presence of God so vitally and in such a real manner as during that tragic testing.

When I had finished the message, I read my resignation. Doug, then Jack, read theirs. We were very brief. We expressed appreciation for the privilege of serving the church and stated that in compliance with the expressed wish of the congregation, we were submitting our resignations. Then I asked the congregation to rise for the benediction.

Grace, Doug, Jack Jones, and I stood at the front, and there occurred an amazing scene. Naturally, the leaders in our ouster were present. They came by, hurriedly shook our hands, and left. They were there, of course, to see for sure that we resigned. It was reported that the chairman of the board and D. K. were so afraid that we might not resign even after the vote of the church that they were going to get a court order to that effect if we did not resign that night. We had resisted their efforts so long that they came to see that the job was well done; and it was.

I cannot forget what the wife of the chairman of the deacons said when she came by to tell me goodbye. In a motherly fashion she said, "I'm so sorry you let this happen. You know you really have great potential as a leader." I could only smile and mumble, "Thank you." But I was thinking that the real tragedy was what had happened to a church that had more potential for far-reaching leadership than any other Baptist congregation in Georgia.

There remained in the congregation more than one hundred of our devoted friends who had suffered with us, and who had felt the nearness of God along with us. I remember that Dr. Ben Griffith made this statement to me earlier: "Tom, I've suffered more, I've been more deeply troubled by this experience than by anything that has ever occurred to me in my life. But, I wouldn't take a million dollars for what I've learned about Christ and his way in this controversy." This statement seemed to express the gratitude that had come to all of us as we felt a new birth of Christian commitment and of the realization of the joys and privileges of a Christian to witness even amidst suffering.

As our friends came by and literally wept on our necks, it was the most tearful scene I had ever witnessed. Grace and I, Doug, and Jack found at the close of this service that our clothes were wet with the tears of our friends. After they had come to speak to us, they clustered together on the front pews and sat there quietly weeping.

Here indeed was the church, crucified and bleeding. These people in less than two years had been vitally awakened to the need of relevant Christian witnessing in our time. By their commitment they had thrust themselves into a situation where they suffered estrangement from friends, and some even from members of their own families. They had learned what it means to be Christian in a time of the confusion of values. The words of Jesus, as recorded in Matthew 10:34-36, were realized: "Think not that I am come to send peace on earth: I came not to send peace, but a sword. For I am come to set a man at variance against his father, and the daughter against her mother, and the daughter in law against her mother in law. And a man's foes shall be they of his own household." Surely, the sword of truth had separated the true followers of Christ from those who would make of the church merely a religious club! These people were now experiencing a new sense of fellowship in the spirit of Christ. Truly we had all become brothers and sisters through this awful experience.

This was the witness that we were making to the world. The important thing was not that 250 people voted against us, but that 189 voted with us and stood with us to make this affirmation. These people came from the same culture as our opponents; yet in the spirit of Christ they had found freedom from their prejudices. Now they were to testify as never before to the reality of the Christian spirit and brotherhood.

I did not weep at this time. My weeping was over. During those awful three months I had wept more than in any other period of my life, perhaps as much as the last twenty-five years of my life combined. I had prayed that through this evening I would have the strength to bear up and to carry on my duties. I felt a strange source of strength as did Doug and Jack and Grace.

When it was over we went home, relieved that the long siege had ended, and that we had passed through the fires maintaining our integrity, being faithful unto the end. We didn't know what tomorrow would bring, but we knew that our lives were more fully in the hands of God than ever before. This was our witness.

13

BEFORE I WAS OUT OF BED on Monday morning the phone
began to ring. NBC News, New York, called for a statement.
I asserted that the house of God must always be open to all
who desire to enter and worship. Representatives of other
leading news media called from New York, Chicago, and
other cities. I repeated essentially the same statement that I
had made to NBC.

The calls came so fast and furiously that I was unable to
shower, shave, dress, and eat breakfast until noon. Grace
was supposed to go to her school but she decided to get a
substitute for the day and remain with me.

WSB-TV, Atlanta, phoned and asked me for a personal
interview, to which I readily consented. The caller informed
me that within two hours a team of newsmen would come
from Atlanta to my home ninety miles away and set up their
cameras in my study. This they did.

The morning newspapers of Macon and Atlanta carried the
story on page one, and we later learned that it was headlined
around the world. In the next few weeks I received clippings
from newspapers in Europe, Africa, and South America.
Reuters, the British news agency, as well as the Associated

Press, and United Press International, had distributed the story.

Here are the Reuters dispatches as published in the *Daily Nation*, Nairobi, Kenya, East Africa; on September 27 and 28, 1966:

"STUDENT EJECTED FROM CHURCH

"Macon (Georgia), Monday. Ushers at a White-only Baptist church in Georgia forcibly ejected a Ghanian student who attempted to attend a service here yesterday.

"Shortly after the incident, church members voted to dismiss their pastor, an assistant pastor, and the church music director who had been pressing for integration."

"BANNED STUDENT PERSISTS

"A Ghanian student who has been forcibly barred from attending a church with Whites says he intends to keep trying.

" 'Missionaries from the Southern Baptist Convention came to my land teaching the word of God, but when I attempted to practice their teaching, I was refused the opportunity in this country,' Sam Jerry Oni said today.

"Oni, the first Negro to attend Mercer University here, was barred from a Baptist Church on the campus on Sunday."

The reader can well imagine what this kind of publicity does for Christian missions in Africa!

Of course, it was the appearance of Sam Oni that bumped the story into international prominence. This was by no means the first time that a Baptist minister in the South had lost his pulpit over the race issue. What was different about this story, however, was that the Tattnall Square Baptist Church minister and his two fellow ministers had taken a clear-cut stand on the issue, had made their position public, had resisted the suggestions of their opponents in the congregation to "leave quietly," and had dared the congregational majority to accept the moral stigma of firing them for their stand.

The news was followed by an avalanche of public reaction. Telegrams, cablegrams, and letters poured in from around the world — the number eventually reached five hundred.

Those that meant the most to me were from ministerial groups in various parts of the United States. Pastors in Macon, Atlanta, and Athens, Georgia; Memphis, Tennessee; Abilene, Texas; and other cities passed encouraging resolutions.

President Harris broke his public silence on the church controversy in a speech to a Baptist Brotherhood dinner in Atlanta. He was quoted in *The Atlanta Constitution,* September 28, 1966:

"The recent trauma at the Tattnall Square Baptist Church of summarily choosing to cut off the life of its ministers, who favored seating a Negro student in its worship service, is not only an act of savagery, but also a denial of the relevancy of Jesus Christ as Saviour in 20th Century life."

Editorials appeared in the secular press. Ralph McGill, Pulitzer Prize winning publisher of *The Atlanta Constitution,* had devoted his page one column to Tattnall Square before our dismissal. Under the heading "An Ineffably Sad Story," he wrote, on September 2:

"Whatever the future of the Christian church is to be, one of its footnotes will be that of a church calling itself Christian, located on the campus of a church-related university, refusing to allow colored students to worship.

"If this were not so ineffably sad it would be hysterically funny."

Eugene Patterson, then editor of the *Constitution,* wrote a daily editorial page column which had won a Pulitzer Prize. Under the heading "Death of a Ministry," his September 27 column began:

"Perhaps the Lord will be more forgiving toward the Rev. Thomas J. Holmes than his congregation was. It is hard to believe he will be scourged from Holy favor for saying, 'I cannot agree to close the door of my church to anyone who wants to worship.'"

Bruce Galphin, a columnist for *The Atlanta Constitution,* went to the heart of the matter in his piece September 29:

"So today Christianity — indeed, any religion — is meaningless unless it can address itself to a universal audience undivided by region or race or wealth or education or station in life."

The *Macon Telegraph* said in its lead editorial September 29:

"History may well record that the great failing of the church in our day was in teaching one doctrine and practicing another, of opening wide the arms of Christian love to all, with certain specified exceptions; and of engaging in hypocrisy when millions of people look to the church as the last bastion of honesty, tolerance, mercy and concern for all humankind."

An editorial in the *Mercer Cluster,* Mercer student newspaper, was bluntest of all. It said: "If God is dead, it's churches like Tattnall Square that killed him." An editorial page cartoon depicted Tattnall Square Baptist Church with the word "Church" scratched out and the word "Club" written over it.

The interdenominational Macon Ministerial Alliance passed a strong resolution supporting our position and drew editorial praise from the *Telegraph* for having the courage to take a stand. Following is an excerpt from the *Telegraph* editorial on October 8, 1966:

"The association lent scriptural power and unified clergy strength to conscience-stricken Maconites struggling to bring their words and deeds into harmony with the Christian ideal.

"The stand may not be popular with some congregations and some ministers. But then the ministry was never intended to be a popular calling. Those who are reviled, may count themselves blessed."

The Negro Baptist ministers of Macon passed one of the strongest resolutions of any group. As the *Macon Telegraph* reported it on September 28, 1966, the resolution stated:

"The reason given for this dismissal was that these ministers had advocated the admission of non-whites to worship in this church. We submit that this action makes a mockery of the Christian ethics to which we pay lip service. The foundation of the Christian religion is laid on the principle of love. First, love to one's God, but equally important, says the Master — love to one's neighbor.

"Men of God pledged and consecrated to the reconciliation of men to God were crucified because they dared to lead their flock into this path. The only characters lacking at this Golgotha were the two thieves, for surely the scorners were there, the haters were there, and our Lord was there being crucified afresh."

Certain of the bolder editors of Southern Baptist state papers took positions on the Tattnall Square episode. Dr. C. R. Daley, in the *Western Recorder* (Kentucky) commended the pastors for their loyalty to the gospel. Mr. J. Marse Grant, in the North Carolina *Biblical Recorder,* noted that it was a waste of mission money for Tattnall Square to endeavor to win converts to Christ in Ghana who would then be refused admission to the Tattnall Square Church. In the *Capital Baptist* (District of Columbia) Editor James O. Duncan took much the same approach, condemning the Tattnall Square Church for hypocrisy in sending mission money abroad and then refusing to accept converts from the mission field as fellow Christians.

The *Baptist Men's Journal,* publication of the Southern Baptist Brotherhood Commission, featured a hard-hitting review of the Tattnall Square episode in the issue of April, May, June, 1967, which won an annual award for excellence.

In spite of these notable exceptions, the vast majority of Southern Baptists simply sat on their consciences and let the discharged Tattnall Square ministers absorb the blow without their consolation. An effort was made by some of the members of the Macon Baptist Pastors' Conference, of which I was a member, to pass a resolution supporting us, but this was blocked by certain leading ministers.

The Atlanta Baptist Pastors' Conference adopted by majority vote a resolution commending the three discharged ministers "For maintaining a Christlike spirit in this matter." Then the majority tried to suppress the action from public knowledge. A report appeared anyway in *The Atlanta Con-*

stitution, page one, Tuesday, September 27. It said, in part: "The resolution was adopted after lengthy debate over the pastors' right to interfere in the autonomous actions of a Baptist congregation. An amendment not to release the resolution to the public was adopted by a two-vote margin, but it was reliably reported that the message supports the stand taken by the Rev. Dr. Thomas J. Holmes, his assistant pastor, Douglas Johnson, and music director, Jack W. Jones."

This story was of comfort to us, of course, but it revealed a very sad situation among Baptist ministers. They felt sympathy in their hearts toward us and yet were reluctant to support our position publicly because of fear of what might happen if their congregations learned of their support. So under the leadership of some of their influential members, the 125-member Atlanta Baptist Pastors' Conference tried to hide their conscientious stand.

The Atlanta Journal carries a daily column of tongue-in-cheek comment under the pseudonym of "Piney Woods Pete." Pete commented on the actions of the Pastors' Conference as follows:

"Dear Mister Editor. It puzzles me that those Atlanta preachers who voted 'overwhelmingly' to back the Macon pastor and his two assistants in their stand upholding desegregation in his church, for which the trio were fired, also voted not to make the text of their resolution public.

"Secrets sometimes backfire. As in the story of the honeymooning couple who didn't want their fellow hotel guests to know they were newlyweds. So they told a porter to remove any rice or scribbles from their luggage and not let their secret out. When they found themselves attracting unusual attention, they asked the porter why he had blabbed.

" 'I didn't tell 'em you was jes' married,' he explained. 'I did jes' the opposite. I told 'em you wasn't, but was jes' good friends.' Yours truly, Piney Woods Pete."

I was to note many times in the months to follow how carefully some of my so-called friends avoided making any public statement concerning what happened at Tattnall

Square for fear they might be classified as integrationists and jeopardize their positions with their own congregations.

Why denominational executives did not come to the rescue of three beleaguered ministers standing for the human right of free worship was explained to an inquiring reporter by Dr. Monroe F. Swilley of Atlanta, president of the Georgia Baptist Convention. The interview by Mrs. Billie Cheney Speed, religion editor of *The Atlanta Journal,* appeared in the Atlanta evening newspaper September 29.

Dr. Swilley was quoted as saying, "The Baptist doctrine of autonomy for local churches makes it impossible for the convention to interfere with the internal operations of a congregation. Officially, that is where it puts us (leaders of the convention). But under our Baptist policy the president of the convention has no right to speak for individual churches."

For example, he said, "In the same city you might find that one Baptist church will have an open-door policy and another might not. This is up to the local congregation. Most assuredly the ministers in the Tattnall Square Baptist Church will be in all of our prayers, hoping that out of this serious matter something may come which will point us toward better paths in the future."

Dr. Swilley pointed out that the Southern Baptist Convention and the Georgia Baptist Convention had made strong pronouncements on the race issue. They have emphasized the universality of the gospel and the freedom of all men to worship God as they are led, regardless of race, color, or creed. But he said that no statement could properly be made by the convention concerning the application of these principles in a specific local church controversy.

Legalistically, this explanation of Baptist polity is accurate, but in fact Baptist general bodies and officials do sometimes intervene in local church matters when they consider the issue important enough. For example, in the fall of 1967 two churches of a Baptist association in North Carolina were practically voted out of the association because of flexible

104

baptismal requirements for new members transferring from other denominations. There was a similar case in Arkansas earlier. In 1953 denominational executives and professors from denominational seminaries testified in court in *behalf of the minority* in the North Rocky Mount (North Carolina) Church dispute over which faction was the true church entitled to hold the property — and the minority won! These exceptions to the professedly inflexible rule of local church autonomy were widely publicized.

It just happens that Southern Baptists are very zealous in guarding the mode of baptism and church property rights, but when it comes to a moral issue of far greater import for the future of the Christian church, they sometimes choose not to intervene. This is the way it is, in spite of the fact that Baptist associations and conventions pass high-sounding resolutions on the race issue that purport to give moral guidance to the churches.

Among the many phone calls that we received the week of September 25, two offered financial help.

A woman phoned from California to say that she and the members of her congregation (not Baptist, by the way) had discussed the situation and stood ready to send financial aid to all three discharged ministers, if needed. I thanked her for her kindness and asked her to convey to her congregation our deep appreciation for their moral support and offer of financial help. I said, however, that we were going to be paid our salaries for the month of October and that at the present time we did not need any money.

One of my dear friends, pastor of a small congregation of another denomination in Macon, called to say that some of the members of his church had asked him if he would investigate our financial need.

These overtures were heart-warming and sustaining to us. Although we did not know what the future held, we decided that we would not accept any financial aid because we did not want anyone to think that we would use this incident to line our pockets. We had taken our stand purely on principle and had determined that we would accept the consequences. We would not profit from it in any way.

In the days that followed, Tattnall Square Church was to be rocked and torn asunder by the shock waves of reaction to the misguided decisions of the majority, but for us the ordeal at last had ended. We were out of it.

14

FEELING WAS STRONG among the students on the Mercer campus after Sam Oni had been turned away from the church door and the Tattnall Square ministers had been forced to resign. Rumors were numerous about what the students might do on the following Sunday if the African returned, as he had promised. University authorities talked with them and asked them to remain calm. Sam Oni, to his credit, refused to allow the students to organize any sort of demonstration. He contended that his desire to return was a personal matter which he had to carry out alone.

At eleven o'clock on Sunday morning, October 2, two Mercer deans were on the front porch of President Harris' home across the street from the church. They were there to observe and to act if any students should try to demonstrate.

Dean Garland Taylor is a tall slender man. At that distance he probably resembles me. Some of the church members looking across the street and seeing these men on President Harris' porch apparently concluded that I was there. Thus a rumor started that I was there, that I had prompted Oni in his two appearances, and that I had arranged for them to be humiliated before the world. Such a charge was to be expected since they persisted in believing that the whole matter was a conspiracy by Mercer and myself to steal the church property.

However, they were wrong in this accusation, as they were in most of the charges they made against us. Grace and I had stayed at home on that Sunday morning. We were exhausted. Additionally, both of us believed that it was not wise that we attend services anywhere that Sunday morning. We realized that our presence in any of the Macon churches would cause comment, and we did not wish to be an embarrassment to any pastor or congregation.

At home we listened to the Tattnall Square services over the radio. The Reverend Robert L. O'Brien was in charge. As the service progressed, we were brought up short by a whispered conversation which was picked up by the sensitive microphone on the pulpit. The church office had received an anonymous phone call stating that a bomb had been placed in the church timed to go off during the morning service. An usher had rushed to Mr. O'Brien and told him that the Police Department had asked that the building be evacuated at once. Mr. O'Brien calmly asked the congregation to evacuate the building quietly but quickly. I felt that this anonymous bomb threat, which proved to be false, was a dastardly prank for anyone to play on the congregation. This further humiliation deepened the sorrow we felt for the now bewildered people. After the members had evacuated the building, the church was searched thoroughly by policemen and church officials. When no bomb was discovered, Mr. O'Brien asked the congregation to return to the building. Most did so, and he somehow finished the service.

The prankster who made the bomb threat was never identified. There was speculation that it was the action of some student. However, I think there are many reasons to believe that it might have been someone other than a student. Even though the Mercer student body had reacted very strongly to what had happened, for the most part the students had shown great restraint and dignity.

There were other acts of harassment of the church by persons who were never identified. Someone painted a sign on a bedsheet and hung it over the church bulletin board on October 2. It read:

"Jesus loves the little children of the world
Red and yellow, black and white,
they are precious in his sight."

I am told that these verses from the familiar children's song were also found written on chalkboards in the church's educational building. During the following week someone placed another sign on the outside bulletin board which read: "Pastor wanted: he need not be a Christian."

The general student reaction was to avoid Tattnall Square Baptist Church henceforth. This was the very thing that I feared would happen. I had pleaded with the leaders, warning them that if the church excluded Negroes, the white students on the Mercer campus would no longer feel welcome. One of the dominant characteristics of the present student generation is their complete contempt for any form of hypocrisy. Their rejection of the shallow elements of institutional religion in our country is almost total. But there is still an appreciation among them of genuine Christianity. I think their reaction is a healthy one and is a hopeful omen for the future.

I knew that we had no opportunity to do anything constructive in leading these young people to find the meaning of life in the Christian faith unless we were willing to give expression to the universal aspects of the gospel. The all-inclusiveness of the gospel is the basis for brotherhood. The tragedy is that the Christian church today, for the most part, has refused to face this fact. Therefore, it has lost much of its appeal to the younger generation.

The violence of the general public reaction to the church's action, both far and near, was a bewildering experience for the congregation and especially for our opponents. They tried to build a defense for themselves in a claim that the race issue was not the central issue at all. It was only a smoke screen, they said. The chairman of the deacons, along with several other men (I do not know their names), went to Atlanta and spent several hours with Jack Harwell, who succeeded John Hurt as editor of *The Christian Index,* and with the executive secretary of the Georgia Baptist Convention. This conference was to explain their side of the controversy which they felt had been obscured in the news stories.

In fairness to all, Editor Harwell agreed to print a story presenting their side if they could provide facts to prove their contention. They promised these facts and returned to Macon to gather them for the editor. When more than a week had passed, Mr. Harwell called the chairman to get the story. He asked for more time and promised the story soon. Weeks passed, and after additional calls, and still no story, the editor gave up on his efforts.

On Monday morning, September 26, a large number of our supporters went by the church office and asked the secretary to give them their letters of membership transfer as they did not wish to remain members of Tattnall Square Baptist Church any longer. They began to look around for a place to meet for prayer and discussion. The assembly room at the Macon YWCA was secured, and word was sent out to our friends that we would meet for a prayer service on Wednesday evening at 7:30. We met at the "Y" for several weeks before finding a more suitable location in the chapel of a sister church.

We assembled on that evening to sing, pray, and talk. There was no evidence of bitterness or hatred. I have never seen such a spirit of brotherhood and comradeship than existed in this wonderful group of Christians. More than a hundred were present. After Doug and I had spoken briefly, we had an informal business session at which it was voted to form a temporary prayer fellowship and to meet on Wednesday nights until a place could be found to meet on Sundays.

The reasons behind this action were mainly twofold. First, the people needed the emotional and moral support of each other at this time. They had suffered much in the conflict with the majority at Tattnall Square Church. None of them felt that they should move immediately into other congregations, and for a time they wanted to let their wounds heal and bolster one another in faith and commitment.

The second reason for the formation of this group was the concern that the financial needs of Jack Jones, Doug Johnson, and myself be met until we found employment elsewhere. It was rather widely reported in the press, both religious and secular, that a new church had been formed. This excited some of the people in Macon, especially some of the pastors, and they began to insist that the Mercer properties not be used by this group. Of course, there was a strong sentiment among some to start a new church in the Mercer chapel. Personally I was opposed to this because I feared that Mercer might be actively drawn into the controversy by such an action. There were letters written to editors and sermons preached saying that Mercer University was behind all of this. I wanted to give no comfort to those who made these charges. Fortunately, we found a place of worship several blocks from the campus.

When the deacons of the church had met on Monday night, September 26, and had voted to accept our resignations and to pay our salaries through the month of October, it also had been agreed that Grace and I could live in the pastorium (parsonage) during the month of October. We learned of these actions only through friends among the deacons. There was never any official notification.

We decided there would be less strain on all concerned if we vacated the pastorium as soon as possible. So we secured an apartment immediately and began packing our household goods to move. This move was the easiest one we had ever made, because a large number of Mercer students and faculty members came to help us pack. They brought station wagons and automobiles and moved our household goods carload by carload to the apartment across town.

Two of the people who helped us move the weekend of

September 30 were Henry Johnson and his wife, Gladys, black people. They told us they had to come to offer their services without pay as a gesture of appreciation for the sacrifice which they felt we had made in behalf of their people. Two of my brothers helped also.

On Monday, October 3, although very tired, I drove to Wake Forest, North Carolina, with Dr. Harold McManus where I spoke in the chapel of Southeastern Baptist Theological Seminary. I was also asked to conduct discussions in several of the social ethics classes. I have never seen on the part of young ministers such a deep interest in any controversy as was manifested in the student body at Southeastern. In chapel I presented a message of faith and hope, refusing to dwell on the bitter and tragic side of this controversy. However, I can never forget a question from one student. He asked, "What hope can you give to young ministers who are preparing to enter the pastorate very soon when we know that if we go and preach the gospel as it is revealed in the New Testament the same fate awaits us which has befallen you?"

Of course, this was very difficult for me to answer. However, I voiced my hope that a new day was coming. If enough ministers will take their stand, eventually the tide will turn. We will see new attitudes born in our churches as the spirit of God works through the witness of faithful pastors and preachers.

Job offers arrived. I had a letter from the president of one of the colleges in the state university system offering me a position as a teacher in the sociology department. Although I felt that I was not qualified to do the job, it was encouraging to know that someone was interested. I had calls from the United States Office of Economic Opportunity in Washington stating that Sargent Shriver, then the national director, had instructed an assistant to contact me and to talk with me about the possibility of my becoming employed in the O.E.O. program somewhere in the United States.

During that month I received two telephone calls from

a Southern Baptist church in Boise, Idaho. The deacons who called indicated that they had checked me out exhaustively, and that the church was prepared to call me if I would accept. I appreciated this compliment very much, but I had decided that I wanted to remain in the South. I had committed my life to doing something in the area of race relations and wanted my ministry to continue in my native region.

In a few days I received a call from President Harris asking me to come to his office. I went and he talked with me about returning to Mercer as assistant to the president for public relations. He stated that he had discussed this matter with the chairman of the board of trustees and with a number of other trustees and several of the faculty. There was a feeling that I could make a contribution to the life of the University.

Of course, Mercer University has a very warm place in my heart. It has meant more to my life than any institution other than my home and my church. Anything to advance Mercer University is challenging to me. Grace and I decided that this was where we wanted to be. We did not want to leave our friends in Macon. So, when the trustees met in October my appointment was confirmed. President Harris announced it to the press, and I returned to Mercer as assistant to the president on November 1, 1966.

What is life like afterward for a minister who has lost his pulpit by bucking the majority in his congregation, and even in his region, over a highly emotional social issue? I never doubted the assurance of a favorite passage of Scripture: "We know that in all things God works for good with those who love him, those whom he has called according to his purpose" (Romans 8:28, *Good News for Modern Man*). But I was to marvel again and again at the way God works to bring good out of evil.

15

A STIGMA is placed upon any minister who is discharged from his pulpit, regardless of the reason, and this tends to isolate him from his brother ministers. There is the implication of failure, whatever may be the circumstances. When the race issue is involved, especially in the South, there is a double stigma — he is considered to have failed in the leadership of his congregation, and he has intruded into an area which even many ministers regard as "off limits."

During my years on the staff of Mercer University before accepting the pastorate at Tattnall Square, I had received many invitations for pulpit supply from churches large and small, not only in Georgia, but in other states. In the vicinity of Macon over a period of four years, I had served as interim supply minister of six churches while they were in search of pastors. Because of my long years of work in the Southern Baptist Convention and Georgia Baptist Convention, I had the reputation of being a good Baptist and denominational loyalist. My discharge from Tattnall Square changed this. Overnight I became a controversial person who was not "safe" to have in one's church. The invitations to preach halted abruptly.

There were old friends in the ministry who remained true. I could name a number in Macon and other Georgia cities. Their steadfastness encouraged me greatly.

President Harris and other Mercer officials were criticized caustically for reemploying me. However, he also received a number of letters from persons across the country commending him for this. The notoriety of my stand gave me an entrée with many people whom I had not been able to reach previously in my work for Mercer University. All in all, however, the rupture of my denominational ties was sharp and painful.

The first invitation I received to speak in any religious gathering following my discharge came from a Jewish synagogue in Macon. Dr. Pierce Annes, the rabbi, came to my office to invite me to preach on Friday evening during National Brotherhood Week. "We feel you know what brotherhood is," he said. I later spoke to an appreciative audience at the synagogue.

In the summer of 1967 I preached by invitation at Woodland Christian Church in Macon for six Sundays following the call of their pastor to active duty in the military chaplaincy. I found many sympathetic friends in this little congregation and deeply appreciated the moral support which they gave me. Also, Mt. Zion Baptist Church, near Macon, invited me to preach a series of four sermons to their young people in the spring of that year. This small rural congregation possesses an unusual breadth of spirit not customarily seen. Perhaps their attitude was due to the fact that through the years Mercer professors had served as pastors of the church.

In the late spring of 1967, President Harris assigned me to direct the development program of the Southern School of Pharmacy, a branch of Mercer University, in Atlanta, at the request of the school's dean and the chairman of the executive Committee of the school. Grace and I moved to an apartment in Atlanta on August 1.

As I plunged into what might be termed "secular" work,

I felt very deeply the isolation from the "religious" community. Sometimes on Saturday evenings and Sundays I felt quite depressed without a place to preach. The major expression of my life commitment seemed to have been stilled.

One day in October, Gainer Bryan and I went to lunch at the Atlanta Press Club. Dick Hebert, one of the reporters who had been excluded from the conference in Macon, arrived at the downstairs entrance of the club as we did and rode up with us on the elevator. He asked what had happened to me in the past year. As I sketched the highlights, he concluded that he would like to do a kind of anniversary piece on the discharge of the Tattnall Square pastor from his pulpit.

Dick came to our apartment, spent about two hours interviewing us, and wrote a rather lengthy article which appeared in the combined issues of *The Atlanta Journal* and *The Atlanta Constitution* on Thanksgiving Day. His mildly exaggerated lead read, "Dr. Thomas J. Holmes is a preacher without a pulpit, a teacher without a classroom, a man wrenched out of the life he had loved." The article dwelt on an ex-pastor's sense of isolation but accurately reported that if he were faced again with the same crisis, he would take essentially the same course.

The appearance of this article opened an entirely new phase of our lives in which God clearly was at work. The account was read that Thanksgiving morning by a Negro minister in Atlanta, the Reverend Walter McCall, pastor of Providence Baptist Church. About 10:30 A.M. when my phone rang, it was Mr. McCall. He told me that he had been so moved by the article that he could not eat his breakfast until he had talked to me. He stated that he and his wife wished to invite Grace and me to their home for Thanksgiving dinner. We were expecting guests for that occasion and had to decline, but I said we would be delighted to come at a later date. He suggested breakfast the following morning. Our daughter and her husband were visiting with us and he included them in the invitation.

The next morning at ten o'clock, the appointed hour, we were at the Negro minister's home. He had invited two of his deacons, Mr. C. B. Fagan and Mr. John Tyler, as well as Dr. Sam Williams, chairman of the Department of Philosophy at Morehouse College, one of Mr. McCall's former teachers. I learned that Walter McCall himself was acting head of the Department of Religion at the College. After a few minutes in the McCall home we felt that we were among old acquaintances. Thus began a friendship that has blossomed in various directions.

When we had finished the delicious breakfast which Mrs. McCall had prepared, Brother McCall began to discuss the newspaper article. "As I read that story," he said, "I began to realize that we black ministers had not adequately supported our white brothers who have lost their pulpits in the fight for racial justice. I knew about your ordeal at Tattnall Square, but had done nothing to show you my appreciation. So I felt I just had to call you and offer you the hospitality of our home."

Walter McCall also invited me to speak at his church the following Sunday morning, and I agreed. This was the first time in many years that I had spoken to a congregation of black people. Pastor McCall introduced me as the minister in the much publicized Tattnall Square Baptist Church story. I shared with those people a sense of rejection, and perhaps that was uppermost in establishing an immediate rapport with them. I talked about some of the things that I had learned in the Tattnall Square ordeal and reaffirmed my faith in the Christian way of life.

Negro congregations have a way of responding vocally to the preacher — "Amen! That's the truth! Preach on!" This gives tremendous support to the speaker. They reacted with increasing fervor to my remarks. After the sermon and final hymn, Pastor McCall began singing with no accompaniment an old spiritual:

> All day, all night, angels watching over me, my Lord.
> All day, all night, angels watching over me.

As the congregation joined him, we all felt a closeness to God that melted us to tears. This experience provided one of the high spiritual crests of my life. I felt the healing balm of Christian love and fellowship in a way that I had not known at any other time. We spent an hour talking with the people after the service. Their warmth, their appreciation of my message, was one of the greatest boosts I have ever received. Grace and I had the feeling that the day marked a new phase in our lives, and subsequent events have demonstrated this was so.

During the next week we discussed the various aspects of our visit with the McCalls and the service in their church. We decided that we must have them come to visit us. So we invited Dr. and Mrs. McDowell, Chaplain and Mrs. Robert B. Herndon, and Walter and Anna Mary McCall to our home for dinner. The McCalls later told me this was the first time they had ever been in the home of white people in the South for a meal. We were concerned about the reaction of our neighbors, but we decided that in spite of what anyone might say or do we were going to have our home open to our friends, whether their skins were black, white, yellow, or red.

The dinner was a time of true Christian fellowship and helped to seal our friendship with the McCalls. Let it be said that not one word or intimation of disapproval has been expressed by any of our neighbors.

As the weeks passed, we talked to each other over the telephone frequently. In conversation with Anna Mary and Walter we determined that our friendship was going to be productive of more interracial communication in Atlanta if we could make it so.

Walter and I met and talked a number of times and decided that we would form an interracial group of ministers for conversation and sharing. We sent out invitations to men of various denominations. We telephoned them, explaining what we had in mind. To our delight we discovered a readiness on the part of both white and black to engage in just such an activity. In the light of this, it seemed strange that there had not been more of this kind of thing in the past. Such relationships seem only to await someone who dares to cross the barriers and move forward.

We usually gathered for lunch at a restaurant, or in a church. We met once in the dining room of the Interdenominational Theological Center as the guests of the Center. These get-togethers featured an honest exchange of points of view and discussion about how we might broaden our fellowship. Walter was writing letters to his minister friends telling them about our service at Providence Church and suggesting that they invite me to preach in their churches. To my delight, I received invitations to the Mount Zion Second Baptist Church, where Dr. E. R. Searcy is the pastor, to the Traveler's Rest Baptist Church, where the minister is the Reverend I. W. Hobbs, and to the Paradise Baptist Church, where Dr. C. Nathaniel Ellis is pastor. Each of these experiences was deeply satisfying to Grace and me.

At this time another strong current was building in Atlanta. Dr. McDowell, who was then minister of teaching at the First Baptist Church, was conducting a Friday morning interracial seminar for ministers. Among those attending were Dr. Martin Luther King, Sr. and the Reverend Benjamin W. Bickers. At Dr. McDowell's suggestion, it was voted to hold one of the seminars during February at the Mount Zion Second Baptist Church and to invite all of the ministers of the white and Negro Baptist conferences to be present.

This was a tremendous occasion! It provided a breakthrough in the interracial fellowship movement. Dr. William Holmes Borders, pastor of Wheat Street Baptist Church, the largest Negro congregation in the Southeast, preached that morning on "Faith." Following his dynamic sermon, more than an hour was spent in discussion of what could be done to bring about regular interracial meetings. Dr. Martin Luther King, Sr., with tears on his cheeks, spoke of the need for this sort of expression of Christian brotherhood and unity in the community. He made a plea that white and Negro ministers unite to change racial attitudes. I told about

119

our interracial discussion groups and urged both conferences to join in such an effort.

Committees were appointed to meet separately and then jointly to make recommendations to their respective pastoral conferences on how we might work out a program of interracial meetings. We had lunch together afterward in the dining room of the Mt. Zion Church. This was a wonderful occasion. I sat with Dr. King, Sr., and we discussed many matters of mutual interest. I saw there the acknowledgment of desires that have long been held secretly in human hearts. I wondered why we are so reticent to give expression to them. Yet upon a moment's reflection it is easy to see that these feelings are held secret because, with the tremendous amount of racism and bitterness and prejudice existent in our country, it is dangerous to express such feelings openly.

The eyes of the world were on Atlanta following the assassination of Dr. Martin Luther King, Jr. in Memphis, Tennessee, April 4, 1968. Violence broke out in several cities of the nation, and the great question was, "What will the home of Martin Luther King, Jr., the place where he was born, reared, and educated, do? What will the people of his race do, and what will be the reaction of the white community in this portentous hour?"

A number of leaders from the religious groups of Atlanta moved swiftly to arrange for Sunday services which would draw the people closer to each other and to God. Mayor Ivan Allen and Police Chief Herbert Jenkins and the forces of the municipal government moved rapidly to calm emotions and to maintain the dignity of this great city.

Grace and I were in constant communication with Walter McCall, and it was decided that we would go to Providence Church on Sunday morning — Palm Sunday — to identify with our friends there in their grief. Walter and I decided that I should make a statement to his congregation. First, he preached, after which I endeavored to speak words of comfort and hope in the emotionally charged atmosphere. Then followed one of the most intensely moving observances of the

Lord's Supper I have ever witnessed. It seemed that something of the tragedy of Calvary was being communicated to us in the crisis of Dr. King's death.

That afternoon Grace and I went with Walter McCall and Bob Herndon to the great Cathedral of St. Philip (Episcopal) on the fashionable north side of Atlanta for a memorial service for Dr. King. Protestant ministers and Roman Catholic priests shared in this service, which was sponsored by the Atlanta Christian Council. The memorial address was given by Rabbi Jacob Rothschild of the Jewish Temple of Atlanta. The great cathedral was crowded with mourning worshipers. Walter McCall and I were sitting in chairs up front just to the right of the chancel. A little Catholic nun was seated beside him. At the conclusion of the service we stood to sing Martin Luther's great hymn, "A Mighty Fortress Is Our God." My white hand was grasping the hymnal on one side, Walter's black hand was holding it in the middle, and the white hand of the little Catholic nun was holding it on the other side. The sacrifice of a black Baptist minister for the truth as he understood it had thus united persons of different races and creeds for a moment of time. I breathed a prayer that such unity would not be limited or temporary, but that it would characterize a new rising of the spiritual leaders of America to rid our nation of racial injustice.

The first joint meeting of the white and black ministers' conferences had been scheduled for Tuesday, April 9. That, however, was the day of the funeral of Martin Luther King, Jr.; so the meeting had to be postponed. It was held instead on April 16, at the Ebenezer Baptist Church, where the fallen leader had served as co-pastor with his father. Dr. Martin Luther King, Sr., was of course present. We sealed our plans for the future that day as we determined that black and white Baptist ministers of Atlanta, representing the largest segment of the city's religious community, were going to work together. As first a black, then a white minister would speak; each one, unconsciously voiced the terms "your group" and "our group." As the meeting drew near the end, Dr. William

121

Holmes Borders arose and asked for the privilege of speaking. He came forward and made the kind of stirring address which is characteristic of this eloquent preacher. He chided the pastors of both races for saying "your" group and "our" group in the discussion, and boomed out, *"We* must act together. *We* can make Atlanta the headquarters of the world. To-gether, *we* can see to it that every child has an adequate edu-cation, that every person has a decent house to live in, that every individual has a job that needs one, that there are better rehabilitation programs for people in the prisons, and that we do everything possible to make this community bet-ter." Pounding the pulpit, he repeated, *"We* can make At-lanta the headquarters of the world. We preachers have the primary responsibility in this cause. Religion is the mother of human culture. We have got to be wise, but we have also got to perform; if we don't, we had better turn in our min-isterial credentials. Dr. King gave his last measure of devo-tion. If we don't give ourselves to the divine task of obtain-ing democracy for the common man, monuments and words will be of no effect." The overwhelming chorus of amens made it clear that he voiced the sentiments of the group.

The joint meetings that were launched that day have con-tinued to offer their share of encouragement that the demon of racism in our midst will yet be cast out and the apartheid movement in our society arrested.

In all these ways God has compensated Grace and me for our temporary losses in the Tattnall Square experience. He has enabled us to sublimate our grief by merging it with that of other broken and bruised members of the human race. The fact that we were willing to suffer for a principle involving love and respect for Negro brothers and sisters has given us an introduction to the black community that we had never had before. The average Negro does not be-lieve in the affirmations of the white community because he has seen too many pronouncements and not enough demon-stration. But where there is evidence of genuine Christian love, black people respond magnanimously.

We violated the mores of the segregated church and paid the penalty, but in the process we were liberated into the larger fellowship of God's people that transcends racial lines. Truly, God has given us "beauty for ashes, the oil of joy for mourning, the garment of praise for the spirit of heaviness" (Isaiah 61:3). Moreover, we now believe that out of the suffering of people across this nation, in which we have shared, there is emerging a redemptive process that spells hope for our fragmented church and society.

Epilogue

HISTORY REVEALS two overriding evils in the system of segregation. The first is the cumulative process of human degradation suffered by the segregated people when they are bound by constant overt and covert procedures through which they are manipulated as things rather than treated as persons. Segregation is impossible without the exerted powers — political, economic, and social — of a ruling class. Second, as the ruling class enforces segregation through the exertion of political, economic, and social power, it cannot escape a concomitant diminishing of its own humanity. This is the two-edged "terrible swift sword" of manifest judgment now striking the American people. I am convinced that through the structures of segregation we have introduced into our society an unintentional nihilism that is slowly eroding all our institutions. This is a prospect too terrible to contemplate for the future of our nation and the survival of the as-yet-unrealized American dream.

As a Christian, I am horrified by the realization that the church, for the most part inadvertently but too often deliberately, has thrown its support to this iniquitous system. It has been correctly observed that the church now faces an internal crisis of ultimate significance — be renewed or die! Can the church be renewed?

The renewals of Christian history have been within the context of the moral and spiritual alternatives of those particular times in which they occurred. Genuine renewal has always been historically relevant. Therefore, we in our time cannot expect spiritual renewal that does not attack the most pressing spiritual problem we face — the loss of man's identity as a person in the image of God. As we lose the meaning of men as persons, ethical values become confused and meaningless. Indeed, when we lose our respect for man, we lose our sense of the greatness of God. The clearest biblical statement of the nature of man, and God's purpose for him in the created order, begins and ends with a paean of praise:

> "O Lord, our Lord,
> *how majestic is thy name in all the earth!"*
> (Psalm 8:1, RSV, italics ours)

In this resulting value vacuum, the awesome powers of men are being turned to self-destruction.

Our all-encompassing technology, the massing of huge, faceless populations, the development of large, rigid, and impersonal institutions, modern nuclear and biological warfare are combining to crush human personality and individuality. To compound this problem, churches have closed their doors in discriminatory acts that further degrade people. Our minds and hearts simply have not been opened to the spirit of Jesus who died for all men.

The New Testament Christians were thrilled to discover that the new fellowship of the church included Jew, Gentile, male, female, slave, master, rich, poor, educated, uneducated. All were reconciled and made one through a new sense of self-respect and love. They were astonished to find that they belonged to a new order of mankind as the image of Christ became manifest in themselves and in those whom they once considered heathen and unredeemable. This

125

microcosm, the church, "the body of Christ," became for them God's pledge of universal redemption and brotherhood. The renewal of the church in our time will mean the rebirth of man's sense of his own value before God, and a consequent redefinition of ethics and morality which will be relevant to our age. When we repent of our inhumanity in the churches; when, in the name of Jesus, we join the struggle to reverse every social process by which our fellows, and we ourselves, are diminished, God's spirit will again blow across our "valley of dry bones" and dispel our despair.

Paul's great peroration on the meaning of the death of Christ, which he saw as both our judgment and our hope, sums up the plea of this book:

"For we are ruled by Christ's love for us, now that we recognize that one man died for all men, which means that all men take part in his death. He died for all men so that those who live should no longer live for themselves, but only for him who died and was raised to life for their sake.

"*No longer, then, do we judge anyone by human standards.* Even if at one time we judged Christ according to human standards, we no longer do so. When anyone is joined to Christ he is a new being: the old is gone, the new has come. All this is done by God, who through Christ changed us from enemies into his friends, and gave us the task of making others his friends also. Our message is that God was making friends of all men through Christ. God did not keep an account of their sins against them, and he has given us the message of how he makes them his friends.

"Here we are, then, speaking for Christ, as though God himself were appealing to you through us: on Christ's behalf, we beg you, let God change you from enemies into friends! Christ was without sin, but God made him share our sin in order that we, in union with him, might share the righteousness of God.

"In our work together with God, then, we beg of you: you have received God's grace, and you must not let it be wasted. Hear what God says:

> 'I heard you in the hour of my favor,
> I helped you in the day of salvation.'

Listen! This is the hour to receive God's favor, today is the day to be saved!" (2 Corinthians 5:14—6:2, *Good News for Modern Man,* italics ours.)